A Letter to My Dog

Notes to Our Best Friends

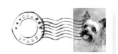

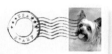

A Letter to My Dog

Notes to Our Best Friends

Photographs by Robin Layton

Created by Kimi Culp, Lisa Erspamer, and Robin Layton

CHRONICLE BOOKS

SAN FRANCISCO

Introduction

The journey and experience of photographing this book has been beyond anything I could have anticipated when the project began. The love that I have witnessed between dogs and their people is all at once intangible and yet immeasurably beautiful: I guess that kind of describes what magic is.

The idea of creating a dog book has been in the back of my mind for years. Having been a photojournalist since 1985, I've photographed a variety of subjects, from a homecoming queen at a local high school to President Obama, from Jennifer Aniston to Oprah Winfrey. Over the years, people have been very complimentary about my photographs, but I have consistently heard them say, "I love your photographs, but I *love* your dog photographs."

Recently, when I mentioned my dream of creating a book of my dog photography while having dinner with friends, one of them, Lisa, came up with the idea of *A Letter to My Dog;* I thought it was genius!

The result has moved me more than I could have imagined: The people I've met and the dogs I've photographed, all welcoming me into their homes with wagging tails (the dogs, too), were pure joy.

For me, the experience is summed up perfectly by these words, from Beth Brown: "I know love, I had a dog."

It has been an honor and a privilege to witness the indescribable tenderness between a person and their dog and to endeavor in my images to preserve magical moments that, I hope, reveal to us anew the beautiful and generous souls of our best friends.

Robin Layton

The Letters

Dear Nike,

It is nearing the end, and your days are numbered. It is an honor and tribute that I write this letter to you, Nike, my true soul mate.

From the day that I picked you up at the rescue at age five, I must have known what an amazing soul you were and were to become, because I named you Nike. You have truly lived up to your name . . . the Goddess of Victory, Strength, and Speed.

You were abused in your previous home before we met but survived in spite of it all. You were mauled by another dog at the age of six, almost bled to death, but survived in spite of it all. You were dropped by a groomer from a high grooming table at the age of nine and suffered a broken back, compressed spine, and blown discs, but you survived in spite of it all. You were so eager to walk and run again after your surgery and you never complained or mourned the loss of your Frisbee days.

Oh, how you flew through the air as you caught every Frisbee that was thrown. What an athlete you were, Nike.

Last year, at the age of fifteen, you survived gastric torsion and the surgery that followed but dealt with a massive stroke twenty-four hours later. This rendered you paralyzed in your hind legs. Within months of all this, you suffered the cruel onset of degenerative myelopathy and grand mal seizures but somehow managed it all. Many say that you should legally be declared a cat because you have more than nine lives. I agree.

Throughout it all, you never complained, always smiled, gained a love of turkey and pasta and, for the last fourteen months, loved the mobility gained in your new cart. You rode it like the true Goddess of Victory assuming the role of Charioteer as you swiftly rode your cart/chariot down the strand at the beach. You greeted all, as the Goddess greeted all with glory and fame. You bring smiles to the faces of many and you are an inspiration to all that you meet. Three weeks ago, a young man looked at you quizzically and remarked to his friend, "Hey man . . . look at that dog." The friend replied, "That is not just any dog, that is Nike . . . she's famous!" I did not even know who they were. People have blogged about you, tweeted about you, put you on their websites, and photographed you. There is even a song about you.

You could not have been more like my own human child if you tried. We both have had reconstructive back surgery, we both have scoliosis, we both are athletes and love pasta and can eat what we want without gaining weight. Despite all our physical challenges, we both are survivors.

In the final moments of our last chapter, darling Nike, we are at the beach. In the last few weeks, you can no longer walk and you are now in a red chariot/wagon. Although tired and weary at almost sixteen (in two months), you still want to eat and drink, watch the waves and the birds, greet every dog, cat, baby, and passerby, and still do not want to give up. You still want to hold your head up high and regal, as you were told your whole life, and have people cheer at you all day long . . . "Just do it, Nike!"

You have done it all, my darling one, and I have loved every minute of caring for you and being your mom. My winged Goddess, may your wings allow you to fly and soar throughout the heavens and my heart forever. I love love love you, Nike.

Mommy

All hail Bjorn, King of Our House! Permit this humble human to sing of your magnificence!

Of nine brothers born in your litter, King Bjorn, you were the biggest. We named you with the Danish word for "bear," to honor your thunderous paws, your deep bass growl, your vast and floppy lips. Soon you would outweigh me, King Bjorn, surpassing all golden retrievers in stature!

I will not speak of certain things, King Bjorn, for I know your self-concept is fragile and your goofiness extensive. I will speak not of the night lightning struck as you were in the yard doing Number Two, how you refused to poop outside for the next six months. I will mention not the lizards and bunnies that slip through your paws on each and every hunt, nor the leaves you must eat to make everyone think you're "just browsing." I'll recount not your mortal fear of swimming pools (you are wise, King Bjorn, to avoid the Demons of the Deep End). No, I will not speak of these things!

Instead I will praise you: your mighty chest, your shining teeth, your fuzzy-wuzziness! I will praise you until my voice gets all squeaky and whistly, as yours does when greeting your subjects! I will rub your tummy until static electricity prickles my fingers. I will sleep with my head pillowed on your velveteen side, unless you have rolled in a dead chipmunk, in which case I will send you to be ministered unto by your Groomers. Blessed am I to have lived in the time of Bjorn the Bear-King. Long be your reign over us, and immortal your memory!

Your loyal subject,
Martha

Dear Happy,

Before I met you, I always thought that happiness was just
an emotion—intangible, not something you could feel or
touch. From the first moment I saw you, I knew that we
would call you Happy and now I know that happiness is also
something that can lick your face, jump up onto your lap,
and run around in excited circles when I come home, and
make me laugh out loud.

I am sorry that there are many times, because of my
schedule and having to travel on the road, that I do not get
to see you for a few days. But I know that the greeting you
will give me when I return home will be the size of a tidal
wave, which is so unbelievable because you only weigh
seven pounds!

I guess I know now that happiness is a thing called Happy!

And that is what you have made me . . .

With love,
Tony

Dear Zoe,

As I type this letter, you are on the floor beside me, always close to me, ready for whatever kind of love I cast your way. You must be made of a concoction of all the cosmic good stuff. You were perfectly designed and we can only strive to be as pure and loving as you, but deep down we humans know too much. You know only to love and to be loved.

I am especially grateful for the lessons that you have taught my children. You teach every day by example. You demonstrate those things that I could never teach. You show them the meaning of unconditional love and forgiveness. You teach them to smile, to jump up and lick someone on the face when they first come in the door, that sleeping is always better with something warm and cozy to snuggle up to, that a long walk and exercise are very good for cleansing the colon, that with just one ball a whole afternoon can be joyous, to be a loyal and pure-hearted friend, and that it feels so good when someone wipes your tears away (in your case, licks the tears away). Maybe most importantly, you teach them that no words are necessary; most of the time, just to *show up* and *be there* is quite enough.

I know these words don't really mean much to you. Words are hollow anyway, and could never be adequate enough to explain our gratitude. So for now it will have to suffice when I give you two pieces of chicken jerky, throw the ball an extra ten times, let you sniff the black wrought-iron mailbox where your friends Mr. and Mrs. Retriever live, take a walk in the mist, and rub your belly . . . always rub your belly. And maybe that's the best lesson of all . . . *show* your love, all the time, everywhere. The only thing that matters is to love and to be loved . . . but you already knew that. We love you Zoe Biggs.

Whitney Biggs, and the little Biggs: Jackson and Marlee

Dear Dorothy (a.k.a. Little D, The Boss, Little Lady),

Even as I type the first few words of this letter to you, my eyes fill with tears.
Tears of joy, that is. In the dictionary the word "perseverance" is defined as
"steady persistence in a course of action, a purpose, a state, etc., especially in
spite of difficulties, obstacles, or discouragement." To me, *you* define perseverance.

When I received the call asking for my help, that your back had been broken and
you were given up by your owners, I feared there was nothing I could do for you.

However, from the moment I saw you limp and lame in that cage, you wiggled
around as best you could and greeted me with so much love, zest, and passion,
I knew you were a survivor.

Our journey began by fitting you with your own mini life preserver to begin warm-water therapy in my bathtub. Your drive from the moment you touched the water was intoxicating.

I still smile when I think of the first day you were fitted for your wheels and how easily you adapted to them. You haven't looked back since. In spite of everything you've been through and all the pain you've endured, you have moved forward with grace and proven resilience.

You have taught me that although life puts roadblocks in our way, you can always go around them or wheel over them and that, although this may be challenging, you will succeed. I watch you approach everyone and anything with this drive that is so intense you are a force to be reckoned with. Most importantly, you have taught me to love big and unconditionally. To be tolerant and nonjudgmental and to accept others as they are.

Dorothy, you are the feistiest, bossiest, smartest, most lovable, cutest, funniest, most persistent, most daring, most giving, bravest little dog I have ever met and I thank you from the bottom of my heart for choosing me to be yours. I want you to know there was no way I could have ever given you up and that one of the happiest days of my life was going from being your Foster Mom to becoming your Mommy.

You have changed my life in more ways than you know and I can't imagine a life without you. The best part of my day is coming home after work to find you waddling your way up to the step and bouncing up and down until I pick you up in my arms for all your sweet kisses. You have touched the lives of many who have met you and most of all me. I love you, D, and all that you are, all that you stand for, and all that you give.

XO
Mom

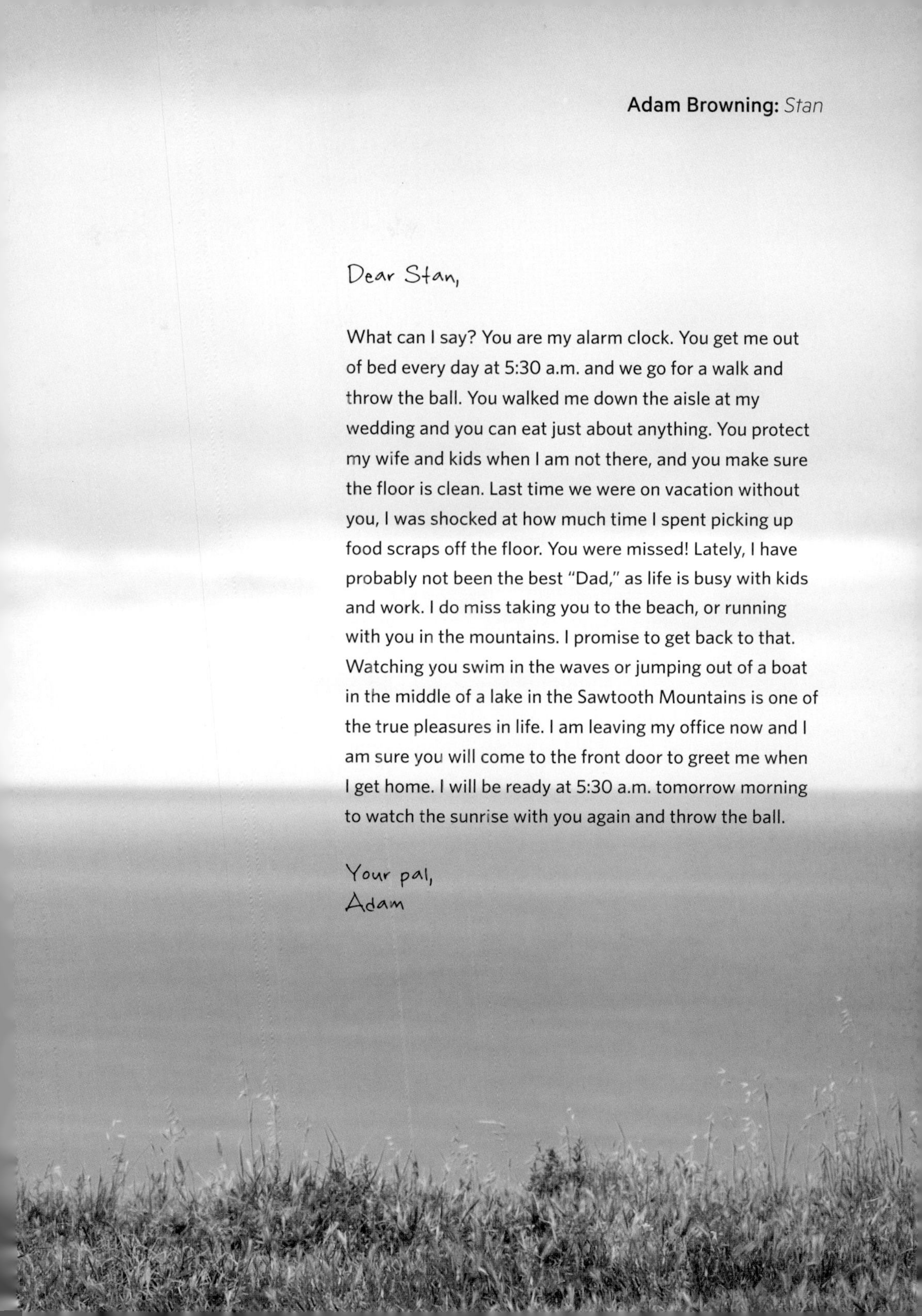

Dear Stan,

What can I say? You are my alarm clock. You get me out
of bed every day at 5:30 a.m. and we go for a walk and
throw the ball. You walked me down the aisle at my
wedding and you can eat just about anything. You protect
my wife and kids when I am not there, and you make sure
the floor is clean. Last time we were on vacation without
you, I was shocked at how much time I spent picking up
food scraps off the floor. You were missed! Lately, I have
probably not been the best "Dad," as life is busy with kids
and work. I do miss taking you to the beach, or running
with you in the mountains. I promise to get back to that.
Watching you swim in the waves or jumping out of a boat
in the middle of a lake in the Sawtooth Mountains is one of
the true pleasures in life. I am leaving my office now and I
am sure you will come to the front door to greet me when
I get home. I will be ready at 5:30 a.m. tomorrow morning
to watch the sunrise with you again and throw the ball.

Your pal,
Adam

Colbie Caillat: *Plummy*

Hi Plummy!

My sweet golden girl! You make me smile more than anyone! I love how any time I pick up my shoes, car keys, purse, or a jacket, you think we are going on a road trip. I love that you're from Taiwan, that your toy rubber ball is your favorite thing in the world, that you love to go swimming in any place where there's water (lakes, rivers, oceans, pools, and even the Jacuzzi). I love that you try to go in the shower with anyone who is getting in one. And how you have a very polite demeanor. I love when we have your beautiful long, blond hair shaved for summer and you look like a puppy again! I love that you like to snuggle, that you wouldn't hurt a fly, unless another dog is trying to mount you: then you turn into "Plum from the streets" and Tae Kwon Do them! And then you go back to mellow, smiling Plummy pawing at me to throw the ball for you. I love your Jacuzzi face where your cheeks hang down and the extra skin on your face droops. I love that you don't bark, ever. I love that when you take a drink of water, it drips from your mouth all the way across the floor to the next room. I love that when we put a leash on you, you jump up and down, grab it, and walk yourself. I love that if someone is holding a towel, you think it's playtime and play tug-of-war with them. I love all of your nicknames (Noodle, Plumper-noodle, Noodski, Noods, Plummer); they are so much fun to say, and you come to all of them! I love that sometimes I find you staring at the wall with a smile on your face, and I wonder, "What is that girl thinking right now?" I love that you know we rescued you, and that you are grateful for the life you have now. I love that on car rides you get so excited that you rub your body back and forth on the seat, and then stick your head out the window and smile while your ears blow in the wind. When we get on the freeway and it's too windy, instead of lying down, you just hide your face. And when I come back to the car, you have moved into the driver's seat sitting up proper like you are gonna drive us home. I love that you are my shadow and will follow my every move. I love that when we got Maté you were so patient with him when he tried nursing on you, sleeping with you, licking your face, and cleaning your ears. You are such a sweetheart. So patient. Thank you for being such a great friend and family member to all of us, Plummy!

I love you sooooooo much!

Maté!

Hi, you little rascal! How come you are so grumpy? You are this fourteen-pound, eight-month-old, messy-haired little punk with so much attitude! Regardless, I love your spunkiness, and how every morning you wait for us to wake up, and then you crawl up on our chests and lick our faces till we have to ask you to stop, and I mean you get up the nose!

You bark at us if we take too long to make your food, you lunge at every dog that passes by us on walks, but in the house you are a sweet little puppy to all our dog friends that come over, and al you want to do is play.

You think Plum is your mom, and it's adorable (but not to Plum!). We call you Oscar the Grouch cause we always find you popping your head out of suitcases with the messiest hair ever, and you are usually grumpy, growling at us, barking or biting. But you also love to snuggle, which makes me so happy.

I love that when I pick you up and lay you over my shoulder you will sleep there for an hour while I walk around the house doing stuff.

I love when we play hide-and-seek around the island in the kitchen. I have so much fun when we play chase in the house or at the park, except for when I drop your leash on walks and try to get you, and you think it's playtime in the street. That's not fun for me.

I love how you will unpack my suitcase as I pack it, take my bras and bathing suit tops and put them in a pile on your dog bed and lie on them. At least you don't chew them up! You collect our shoes from around the house; some are too big for you and you trip when you're running away with one; it's hilarious.

Your nicknames are Tater-tot, Lots-of-mots, Tay-tay, Maté-laté, Oscar (when you're grumpy), and Penny (cause that was your mom's name and sometimes you look like her).

I love that you are such a good tour dog, and so great on the bus! You are pretty good at getting baths, and when we blow-dry your hair, you look like you're in a 1980s rock band. You are too cute for words and, even though you upset me sometimes,

I love you with all my heart and look forward to seeing you every day!

Kim Carney: *Pixel*

Dear Pixel,

We weren't ready for a puppy. It was too soon after our beloved cocker spaniel, Scooter, passed away after a long illness. His loss left a big hole in our house. My husband, mom, son, and our Chihuahua, Pica, all felt profound sadness. Occasionally, a tuft of Scooter's long, black hair would scoot across the floor and we would all tear up.

A friend emailed me a link to a teeny, tiny rescued Chihuahua-mix pup. "OK," I said, we would just go have a look, just a look, but we were not bringing a puppy home. After I filled out the paperwork, collected our driver's licenses and checkbook (just in case), we all crowded into the car to meet you. My husband wondered if we would need our passports to prove citizenship.

When Rebecca met us at the door, we didn't even notice the tiny bundle in her hand. And suddenly, there you were. You could not have weighed much more than a pound. You looked straight into my eyes. I'd never seen a dog look at me so directly and intently. My mouth opened and these words fell out, "Am I your mommy?"

Out came my checkbook and away we went with you cradled in my coat to protect you from the cold. We named you Pixel because of your size.

You were so small that we carried you up and down the stairs to go outside. We never left you outside alone because you were so vulnerable. You were afraid of everything: the rain, the wind blowing a leaf, a crow's shadow. Really, it was your dad who carried you everywhere with him. Your tiny paws hardly touched the ground your first couple of months in your new home. You two loved to watch baseball games and take short naps together.

It didn't take long for you to develop quite a ferocious personality in the safety of your home. You would do that ninety-mile-an-hour sprint in a circle around the house for hours, then slip into the sofa pillows for a nap. But your favorite pastime was stealing treasures and hiding them behind the sofa. It was your lair, about five inches deep with stolen goods. No one's purse was safe in your presence, and we advised all innocent visitors not to leave them open or on the floor. You loved to take chewing gum, breath mints, pens, pencils, paper, checkbooks, and lip balm.

Remember those expensive, hooked-wool decorative pillows that you chewed up into little bits? And when the shoe repairman told me I should feed my Chihuahua, because you kept chewing my favorite leather sandals?

And the time you stole chocolate from a friend's purse and ate it, foil wrapper and all? We had to spend a long night at the emergency vet, didn't we?

Well, all is forgiven because watching you play hard and grow up, the cuddles, the big kisses, and our hearty laughs are great trade-offs. The funny thing is that you rescued us, not the other way around.

Your biggest fans and devoted family.

Archie to me is a sign of hope, love, compassion, and relief. When I see Archie, it makes all my problems go away and fills me with love and hope that everything is going to be OK one day. I can only hope that Archie means this way to all of us at Casa. And this is what Archie means to me, and I hope you all feel the same way I do about Archie the hero dog. The End.

Chris (age 11)

The first thing I have to say is I'm in this placement, I miss my family. He means a lot to me, he feels like a family member to me. He helps me cope. He is a very good friend to me. He feels like a dad which I really wish I could know him. Archie also helps me when I'm sad. I can count on him. I can talk to him like a family member. Love,

Amy (age 11)

To me, Archie is a friend who doesn't judge me or care what I look like. He is always there when I need him. If I'm having a bad day, I can always rely on Archie to cheer me up. When you need a hug, he's there too. When you're feeling lonely, you can take him on a walk; that always helps. If he slobbers on you, it's OK, it means he loves you.

Tyler (age 17)

The first time I met Archie, I was so excited, I couldn't be happier. He was so big, I couldn't believe it. Even though he drools a lot, I still love him Archie is my best friend; I would love to visit him every day. I wish Archie could live in the same cottage with me. Archie is the most wonderful therapist dog I've ever met. He is so cute and fun to swim with in the pool.

He is so adorable. Everyone loves Archie; there is no one that hates him. But what Archie means to me is that he is just like my family, because I never had a real family especially there for me. He is always there for me when I'm upset, mad, etc. He means a lot to me.

I really appreciate that he is here for us.

Kimberley (age 14)

Dear Madeline,
a.k.a. Maddie a.k.a. Maddles a.k.a. Maddie Cakes!

You came into my life when I needed someone to take care of.
I soon learned that we would be taking care of each other.
You have brought me such love, friendship, and just plain ol'
happiness.

   You helped me start Maddie's Corner, and because of you,
I have wanted to help other animals who deserve love and a
happy, healthy home. Thanks for picking me. I hope I'm as good
a mama as you are a baby. I couldn't love you more if I had
given birth to you myself!

Love,
Mommy

Dear Harlow,

You're a part of our crazy, loud, active, busy family and could never be replaced, our sweet rescued girl.

I wanted to write you this letter to let you know how special you are to all of us. The whole family loves to snuggle with you, cuddle with you, take you with us on road trips, and even quick trips in the family car to the grocery store.

We can fit you in our bike basket when we cruise down to the beach and run around in the sand with you until you get too cold and need to be wrapped back up in the safety of your blanket.

We love to nap with you and play in the backyard with you, and we love to giggle watching you go flying as we jump on the trampoline together.

However, I'm so sorry we're not home enough to do even more of this with you. I wish we weren't so busy all the time, running all over town taking care of the little things that seem to fill up the days. I'm sorry the boys are in school all day, five days of the week, and I wish I wasn't off working somewhere out of town, away from you.

We love you and hope you know it, even though we aren't around as much as we'd like to be to enjoy all the fun things we vowed we'd do with you when we brought you home from the shelter.

Love,
Cat xox

Dear Mokie,

The other night when we were in bed lazily watching a television show, you unexpectedly jumped into bed and onto my lap, and you are not small. It appears the fire alarm in the show was making you nervous so we shut off the program and allowed you to sleep stretched out among us. As half my body dangled from the bed (a queen, by the way), I felt you relax and then I felt you pee on me because you are incontinent in your old age. And yet, despite this extreme discomfort and the fact that you smelled like a three-month-old sponge after a weekend of swimming, I wouldn't have dreamed of kicking you off. That is just how much I love you.

I am so comforted by your presence everywhere I go. You even sit right outside the tub as I take a shower, a sight that I cannot seem to get over no matter how many times I see it. I love to hear that contented sigh before you drift off to sleep. I know how much you love me, but I recognize that it is our son Vincent you are interested in protecting most. For this, I am indebted to you. I will even forgive you for your loud barking and waking him from his nap, because I know you are just doing your job. I apologize heartily if unkind words have been said to you in anger!

Sometimes, when we climb the stairs of our apartment, I can read the trepidation and pain in your big cow-eye expression. I know those stairs are beginning to hurt you a little and it hurts me too because I know you are an old girl and you are slowing down. Don't fret, Mokie, there is no amount of money that I won't spend on Adequan shots for you. And there will be a day when you are not by my side anymore. It is a thought too hard to bear, but your memory will live on and so will the fur that you have shed on all our clothing and furniture. I intend to honor you by not vacuuming. But for now, you are here panting your sweet perfume breath in my face and I feel like the luckiest girl in the world.

I love you!

Fran Drescher: *Esther*

Dear Esther,

I love you with all my heart. You are a light from God.
An angel. You don't have a mean bone in your body.
I am blessed to have you in my life.

 You taught me a great life lesson: that you can love, lose,
and love again!

 Thank you for that, my darling girl—you are a magical
creature and I witness you as you cast your loving spell on
all who cross your path.

 I love you, Esther. Don't ever leave me.

Always,
Mama
xo

Dear Sammy,

You are soft and cuddly, good at listening and very energetic. You are one of my best friends. You don't try to hurt people.

If you see new people, you want to meet them. Sometimes you jump, but normally you're just all hyper and run around people.

We play games together. We play chase, Frisbee, ball race, and we occasionally bonk heads. You are a good wrestler, but most of the time we can't catch you because you are so fast.

You are super-soft and make a very good pillow. At night, when we are watching TV, you let my brother Owen and I lay on you and you stay put. Your tickle spots always change. You shake your leg back and forth. I love when you really have an itchy spot and want attention and you lay down or come up to me.

Owen likes petting you and throwing things to you. You are so smart—because you bring things back. We don't ride on your back because it might hurt you.

You are one year old and a fantastic dog.

Love,
Ethan

DuBois,

If only I could speak "DOG" for a day, there would be so much to bark about!

I would share how much I needed you when you came into my life, although it may have seemed you needed me.

I'd tell you how much I love your big brown eyes and let you know what a stud muffin everyone thinks you are!

I would thank you for being so gentle with the other little pups.

I'd tell you how much happiness and laughter you have brought to me with all your silly quirks, and describe the comfort I feel when walking into my house knowing you are there to greet me with your happy tail!

I am blessed to have such a special DU-MAN (half dog/half human) in my life and couldn't dream up a better dog!

I love you forever!

Chet Frith: *Gunner*

Dear Gunner,

You entered my life at such a trying time. I had just returned from a year in Iraq. The world I had known before, my entire life, no longer existed. Life in a combat zone had become normal for me. And this great country, along with its freedoms and liberties I fought to protect, had become so foreign. I was emotionally numbed by my experiences and could not tell you what I enjoyed in life anymore. I left my beautiful wife, and two young boys, all of whom I so desperately loved, only to return unable to feel or express my deep love for them. I felt my world was falling apart around me and I didn't know why. I didn't feel safe anywhere. Going to the grocery store, my children's school . . . even a simple walk in the neighborhood was mentally exhausting. I had recurring nightmares that bothered me long after they had ended. I desperately needed help.

And then you arrived and gave me hope. You have my back everywhere we go and make me feel safe in places I once avoided. You remind me every day that there is good in this world and that there is love. You show me how to forgive and forget, and help me relax in times of stress. Most importantly, you bring a ray of sunshine to my family and me. You mean the world to us! While words can never truly capture how important you are, I want to say thank you, Gunner, my friend.

With every gentle nudge and with every attentive move, you help me realize that, while combat is horrific and will always be part of my life, as well as the lives of all service members who've answered the call of duty, it does not define who we are.

Chet Frith
Lieutenant, US Navy, Naval Hospital Jacksonville, Florida

Stormy,

Your dad, who happens to also be my husband, has often accused me of loving you more than him. While I have denied this for some years, I finally had to tell him that, yes, I do love you more.

Things would have been different if he had run to the back door to greet me whenever I came home, jumped up and down whenever I wanted to go for a walk, sat quietly and attentively waiting for dinner no matter what I was cooking, come immediately whenever I called his name, and/or happily watched all my favorite TV shows while licking my legs. It was really quite simple. Oh well, yes! I do love him. Just not as much. You sweet thing.

Love,
Mom

Dear Chunk,

That's what my life's come to now . . . writing a thank-you letter to my dog. I have to admit I don't completely get this whole thing. I thought you were supposed to write a thank-you letter after someone gives you a gift. Like a Ms. Pac Man machine. If anything, Chunk, I feel like you should be writing me a thank-you letter. But since you're not registered anywhere, I don't even know what kind of calligraphy pens you're partial to, never mind letterhead. I guess I'll try to get through this.

Thanks for letting me put those stupid bandanas around your neck when you get back from the groomer. I know you don't agree, but it really adds to your personality. It's blatantly incongruous to your aloofness and, for that alone, you should be lauded. Thank you for being my only dear friend who has never actually spoken. Thank you for guarding the house. Thank you for letting me tell you lies . . . like the time I told you "thank you for guarding the house." Thank you for not taking shadoooies on the floor. Thank you for having good table manners. And thank you for not being a cat.

I knew you were my dog the minute I laid eyes on you, and I know you knew the same (even though it was my assistant who picked you up from the pound). So, I'll say it once more. Thank you for making me a mommy. You will always be my main man.

Keep this letter safe; you'll probably never get another one. If I could complain about one thing though, I really wish you had opposable thumbs so you could play Ms. Pac Man with me. That . . . would be a real gift.

Love,
Chelsea

Jackie Hassine: *Oliver*

Oliver (Ollie, Oliver Einstein, My Muppet, My Noodle,
My Sweet Pea),

I marvel every time I look at you, and wonder who you are (what planet did you come from?). You are human, part stuffed animal, a whimsical, comical cartoon character (a Jim Henson creation?). You are all heart, covered in strands of long, blond fur, and I love you more than words can express.

My sweet Jasper had just passed away after battling a rapid, aggressive cancer. It happened in just two months. My Max and I were devastated, and I was definitely not ready to think about getting another dog.

When my parents asked me to take them to adopt a dog just five days after Jasper passed, I wanted to say no. But I didn't. In my mind, there was no logical reason why I would end up at animal services that day, so soon after losing Jasper. It was really hard, but I wanted to help my parents. I took them through the shelter with tears streaming down my face as I said "hello" to each dog, in each cage. My parents put their names on a few lists for particular dogs they were interested in, and I was grateful when we were finally heading home, back out down the long corridor to the entrance.

We were almost to the exit, when we passed a side corridor where they were bringing in a new dog; it was YOU! Something made we walk over to say "hello." You were a matted, dirty, skinny mess, but within moments I wanted you. I put my name next to yours on a list and went home. They hold all homeless dogs for five days and I thought for sure someone would come to claim you. No one did.

Lucky me.

You make me laugh every day! Whether it is at the pond or in the yard, when you are running full speed and then doing a nosedive into a somersault for no apparent reason, you just crack me up! And when you stand and walk on your two back feet to get a better view over the bushes, you are like a nosy neighbor.

You are too much, Oliver!

You are loved by people and dogs alike. You have so many friends; I think your social life is busier than mine.

You are the only dog I've ever known who will take a cookie and then save it for later. Sometimes you even wait until I get back from running an errand and you greet me at the door with it. It's like you want to give me a present for coming home. But in reality, you are MY gift, Oliver. I love your big, black nose and your expressive eyes that glimmer with light and love and life. I love that your sweet funny face is the first thing I see every morning when you jump up on the bed to cuddle and the last one I see when I kiss you goodnight on top of your head and wish you sweet dreams. Thank you for the joy you are in my life and all the ways you make our house a home.

XXXOOO
Your mommy

Mariel Hemingway: *Bindu*

Dear Bindu,

You are small and you are big . . .
You are skinny and you are mighty . . .
You are greasy and you are regal . . .
You are lazy and you are tireless . . .
You are a little monk in a dog body . . .
You are forever my true and dedicated friend . . .
You have curled up next to my trembling heart through .
the toughest of times . . .
You have whistled and snored your way into my being . . .
I would not be fully me without you . . .

I love you, Bindu,
Mommy

Buddha, my senior-citizen fur child,

It's almost thirteen years now that you have been with me
on this planet called Pug.

Who knew when I took you home at five and a half months
that you would shed enough to clothe an entire planet.

You are blind now and you teach me every day what
it's like to live without your sight. You have to navigate
around your wife, Little Miss Black Pug Sabina; Otis, a much
younger pug/terrier; and Bubba, a Chihuahua.

You are my mentor for my own journey of aging. I will
be with you every step, as you walk down the path of your
life. I am grateful that I will be able to help you get to the
other side when you are ready. I love you, my little blind
boy Buddha.

You have given me more than I could ever give you.
One day, when you are on the other side, I will look for short,
sticky, fawn pug hair and roll myself around in it in LOVE!

Long live planet PUG!

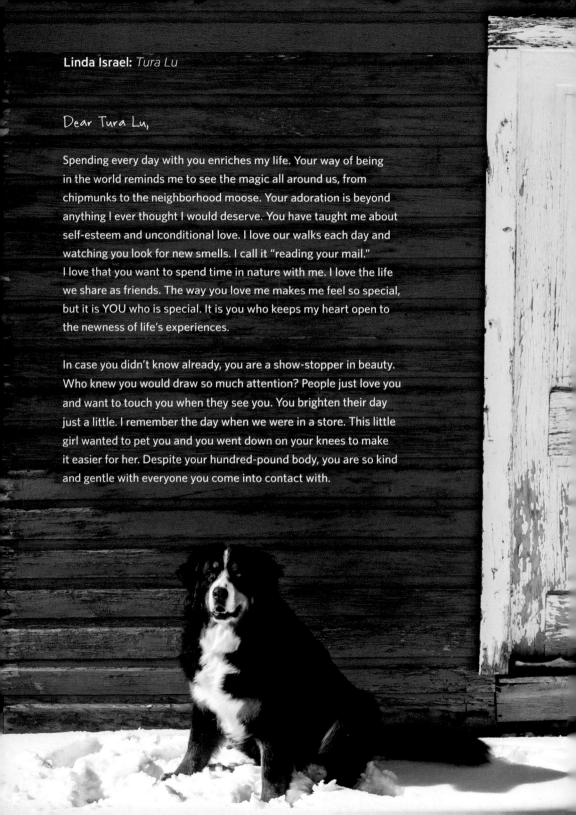

Linda Israel: *Tura Lu*

Dear Tura Lu,

Spending every day with you enriches my life. Your way of being
in the world reminds me to see the magic all around us, from
chipmunks to the neighborhood moose. Your adoration is beyond
anything I ever thought I would deserve. You have taught me about
self-esteem and unconditional love. I love our walks each day and
watching you look for new smells. I call it "reading your mail."
I love that you want to spend time in nature with me. I love the life
we share as friends. The way you love me makes me feel so special,
but it is YOU who is special. It is you who keeps my heart open to
the newness of life's experiences.

In case you didn't know already, you are a show-stopper in beauty.
Who knew you would draw so much attention? People just love you
and want to touch you when they see you. You brighten their day
just a little. I remember the day when we were in a store. This little
girl wanted to pet you and you went down on your knees to make
it easier for her. Despite your hundred-pound body, you are so kind
and gentle with everyone you come into contact with.

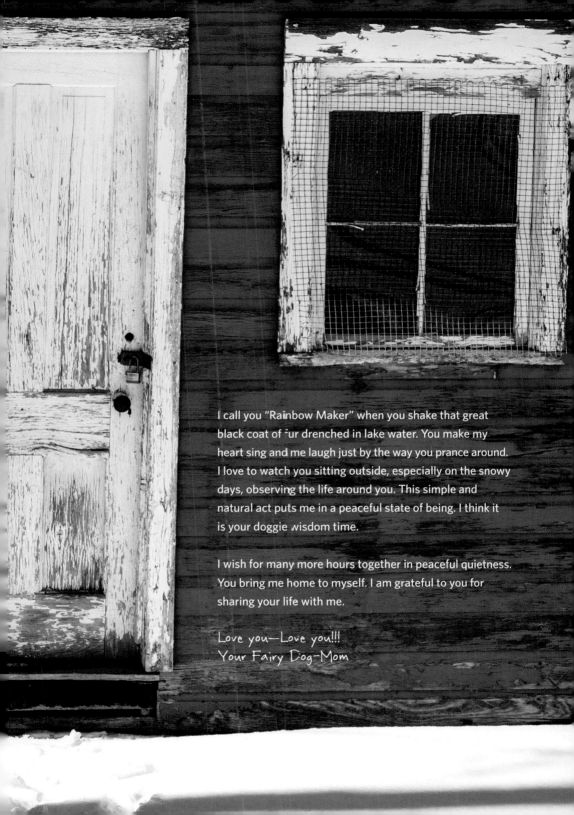

I call you "Rainbow Maker" when you shake that great black coat of fur drenched in lake water. You make my heart sing and me laugh just by the way you prance around. I love to watch you sitting outside, especially on the snowy days, observing the life around you. This simple and natural act puts me in a peaceful state of being. I think it is your doggie wisdom time.

I wish for many more hours together in peaceful quietness. You bring me home to myself. I am grateful to you for sharing your life with me.

Love you—Love you!!!
Your Fairy Dog-Mom

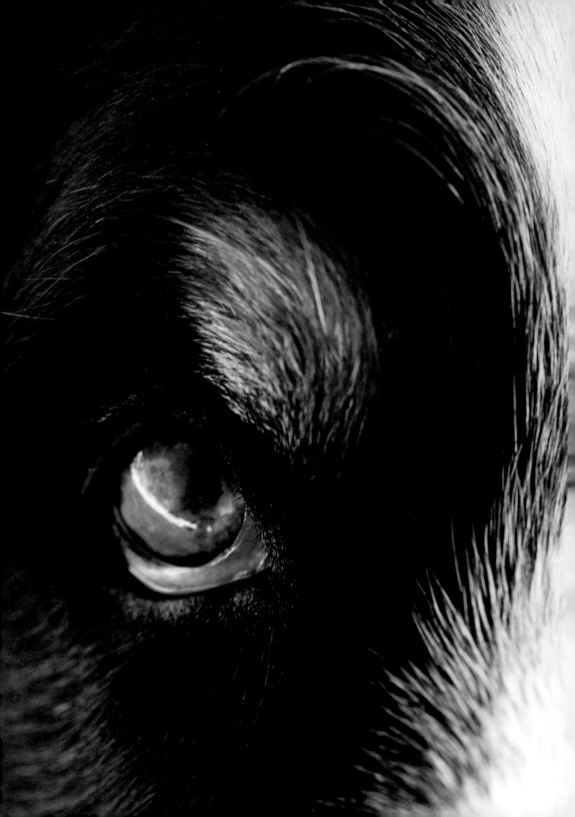

Dear Cooper/Coop/Coopy/Coops,

Where do we start? Your name was Hollywood before we adopted you and you have never ceased to live up to your original moniker. You were the star of our building and, when we moved to a new home, our neighbors knew your name before they knew ours. Who can help themselves when they are greeted with that wagging curly-q of a tail and wiggling rear end? Only to be wooed further when you ever-so-gracefully plop yourself on the ground, belly up, tongue flailing, those big, brown bug-eyes pleading for just one rub? We all know you're a human trapped inside a canine's body. It's apparent from your wrinkled expressions and sideways looks that you're trying to tell us that you should really be standing on two legs instead of four. But we wouldn't have it any other way, despite the fact that you snore so loudly that it wakes the baby, that you shed so much, and that you hate the rain with such a passion that we inevitably, later on, find a surprise from you, hidden discreetly inside the house. But your flaws are few and far between compared to your positive qualities. The way you shower everyone with kisses, run to the baby's side when she lets out the littlest whimper, and think you're a lapdog, although at more than thirty-five pounds you're one heavy package. And it's all because the amount of love you have to give is endless. It's unconditional. It's palpable. It's larger than life, and it's why we love you more than you will ever know. I could go on forever about your infinite charming characteristics but you keep placing your paw on the return key, which is making it impossible for me to type. We are so lucky to have found you, little man; you will always have a special place in our hearts.

Love, Momma, Daddy, and Baby Two

Emily Kraper: *Palmer*

Dear Palmer,

You have not been a member of our family for long, but now that you're here, there is a distinct feeling that something significant was missing before. When we saw you for the first time at a mere four weeks old, we knew you were the one. Your father was won over by the white wisp of fur on your right hip, your eager appetite, and the fact that you were a shameless back sleeper, while I simply looked at you and had a feeling.

Since the day you came home with us on June 26, 2011, our days have been filled with more laughter, love, and affectionate dog kisses than we could have known we were missing before. Between your insistence on barking with a baseball in your mouth, your newfound love of hunting and gathering sticks at 6:00 a.m., finding your voice through awkward howls that both scare and surprise you, and the frantic, chaotic excitement that erupts when someone utters the words "chow, chow," you are constantly finding ways to make me laugh, especially when I need it most.

Perhaps the thing I love most about you, however, is the way that you look at me: with complete trust, a gentle reassurance, and a quiet protective (but not possessive) loyalty. Without trying at all and without looking too hard, you are able to see the best version of me. To you, it is right in front of you and is the only version of me you can manage to find. You fail to notice my clothing, my profession, or my pedigree, and you love me wholeheartedly anyway; you only have to make eye contact for me to understand that you love me and you trust me to make the right decision. Your trust in me is that generous, that encouraging, and that selfless.

Thank you for making me laugh, for throwing all your body weight on my back in the morning in an effort to cuddle, for ensuring that I never dance alone in the kitchen while making dinner, for being so excited to see me each time I come home, for so enthusiastically seeing the best in everyone and wanting to greet them accordingly. To simply say "I love you" falls short of how I feel, but I am hopeful that I can make it up to you in tummy rubs, frequent trips to the beach, and sharing my pillow and the occasional piece of chicken from my plate.

Our family was incomplete without you, and we can only thank you for the ways in which you've blessed our lives to date. We can only look forward to the many laughs and memories to come.

Love, Your mom

Jennifer La Farge Perry: *Bailey Mae*

Dear Bailey Mae,

Your given name may be Bailey Mae, but depending on the rhythms of the day you go by Shrimp Toast, Cheeky Cheeky Bull, Little Pooper, and Schnugums.

Your favorite pastimes:
Visiting each outside door to determine our whereabouts and emitting the most poignant squeak when we have been discovered. Systematically moving everything off the kitchen table into the backyard . . . and then bringing all of the backyard into the kitchen. Wreaking havoc with cardboard boxes in the toniest boutiques in Santa Monica. Fixating on any flying object. Flatulence.

Your beloved spots:
Laps, crooks of knees, towers of pillows, anywhere with waves, expensive store carpets (excellent for self-propelled belly rubs), any Fairmont Hotel (this may be an acquired taste).

Your best traits:
You have the stance and stamina of a horse . . . can toss off a six-mile run on those mighty sixteen-inch legs. You worked right through the projectile vomiting on your last photo shoot. You have a soft spot for old men with hats, as many of them, due to the wisdom of their years, carry dog biscuits . . . and an affinity for the tattooed, somewhat toothless guys in the rehab on the Venice Boardwalk. You are a Democrat. Some days you are definitely smarter than my children. You greet everyone like they are a long-lost friend.

Your doggedness:

You were a gift to our youngest daughter for her eighteenth birthday . . .
and have returned that gift in spades. Our daughter is engaged in a Herculean
struggle against addiction, and your plucky, steadfast little self has been there
for her and us every step of the way. There are many days on our journey toward
healing that an upward glance from your limpid, brown eyes and that little bee
dance you do with your back half when you are welcoming us home are the
tonics that clear the way for another day. In short (and that you are), you are
twenty pounds of happiness.

Jennifer

Dear Monkey,

I thought I was the one rescuing you, but I would quickly learn that it was you who rescued me.

After picking you up at the shelter, I couldn't believe how fast you got into my heart. In all my life, I've never seen a dog with so much character, so much personality, so much life. I knew you could never replace my beloved Ali, who would have been your big sister, but you showed me I could love again.

People stop me all the time and say, "She is so cute, what kind of dog is she?" and I proudly proclaim, "She's a one-of-a-kind!"

Thank you for giving me a reason to make up ridiculous songs and sing them to you, for letting me kiss your face a thousand times a day, but, most of all, thank you for reminding me of the unconditional love a dog can give.

I love you so,
Robin a.k.a. Mom

Dear Albert,

Our little stray from the shelter! If you could speak,
I'm sure you'd say what I do . . .

When you adopt an animal, you create a little miracle.
You right a little bit of what's gone wrong on this hare-
brained planet of ours. You feel like every superhero rolled
into one, because you took something dark and awful and
made it right again.

We love you forever!
xo Mom

Dear Daphne,

Originally, I was looking to rescue a cat when I spotted your big, brown eyes peering out from a cage. The rescue worker said you were found in a box on the side of the street and hadn't had all your shots yet. So, if I wanted to see you, I would have to hold you: "Hold the puppy." That was it. You wrapped your paws around my neck and put your head on my shoulder. I knew we were going to be best friends.

When my brother passed away, you slept beside me and were literally my tissue box as I cried into your furry side every night. One night, I said aloud that you probably had no idea what a comfort you are to me, and you put your paw in my hand. I'll never forget that moment.

We've had so much fun running at the beach, dressing up for holidays (although this may not be your favorite), and taking long afternoon naps. You've met all my boyfriends and greeted them all kindly, even though you were probably not that impressed.

You are my Baby Girl, Snuggles, Dafferdoodle, and I love you very much.

XOXO, Me

Armando Martinez: *Roscoe*

Roscoe is my dog. I like him and he likes me.
He gives me his paw and does not bite my hand.
He runs with me, jumps on me, and he grabs me.
He keeps strangers away. His bark is loud and funny.
Roscoe is a big dog. He snores a lot and yawns.
He gets happy when I get home, so I give him a kiss.
We grew up together. He is five years old.
He kind of looks like me. I like running up the hills
with him. He is my favorite dog. I love him because
he does not eat people.

Armando

Dear Sparky,

This letter is long overdue. It is a love letter, dear dog, from your mother. Just why I took to calling myself "Mommy" in reference to you is a bit of a mystery. I suppose it was because Spencer decided you were his brother and since I am his mother . . . that made me . . . well, you get the picture.

I read a poem once, I long ago forgot where, which professed to explain a dog's thoughts . . . it went like this:

Are you gonna eat that?

Are you gonna eat that?

Are you gonna eat that?

I'll eat that.

And while there is a certain food-centric quality to some of our dealings (you want it, I have it), what we have is so much more than that.

For the eight years we have lived together, there has not been one moment of one day when you have failed to look at me with eyes of love. John, the doorman at our apartment building, calls you "the smiling dog." You do seem to smile with a deep inner light. My father, a wise man who could not take a walk without every dog in the neighborhood following along, used to say, "A dog sees his God."

So I would amend the poem above for you, Sparky. Here's what I think you're thinking:

Do you love me?

Do you love me?

Do you love me?

I love you.

If that's right, Sparky, then I want you to know, I do indeed love you. And if it really is just more of last night's roast chicken that you're dreaming of, then that's coming, too.

Thank you Sparky,
Love, Mommy

Dear Athena,

I was doing a story on puppy mill abuses for the *Today Show* when volunteers told me about a large standard female poodle who was beaten within an inch of her life by the cruel puppy mill owner. A brave worker managed to get her, broken-nosed and bleeding internally, to a shelter where she was operated on, received over sixty stitches, and survived. Just as the tragic story was concluding, the chin of that very same poodle rested onto my lap. That poodle was you. I named you Athena, fitting to the goddess you are, and we've been together ever since. And though I'm so sad over your first seven years, living at the puppy mill, outside on a cement floor in an overcrowded kennel enduring northeast winters without heat, bonding time with your many litters, grooming, care, or love, I'm happy to know that these last six years you've had doggy brothers and sisters, a mom and dad, and Greek grandparents who love you so much. We're all sorry we couldn't have been there sooner, but we are so blessed to have you in our lives now.

I love you, big girl!

xoxoxo
Mommy

Anna Mialky: *Crosby*

Dear Crosby,

You're the best friend anyone could have. There are so many ways you are special to me. Like when I'm upset, you're always there, no matter what. I know I can always count on you.

You are so sweet, loving, playful, and sometimes getting into trouble! There is nothing that could replace you. I love when you roll onto your belly and give me a big, slobbery lick.

I had to beg my parents for more than four years to get us you. No matter how much trouble you get in, I will always love you.

Love,
Anna

P.S. You look beautiful when your pretty fur coat flows in the wind. Also, please stop eating my socks.

Sarah Mortellaro: *Sammy*

Dear Sammy,

I am so glad you're my dog because, whenever I'm feeling
down, you come over to me and put your head on my shoulder.
Whenever I'm mad, you give me a nudge with your nose.
If I'm sitting, you'll come sit in my lap. Sometimes when I am
bored, you come over to me with a ball in your mouth.
It makes me laugh. One day when you ran away after a truck,
I was so sad. I thought, how am I supposed to live without
you? Then we got in our car. We couldn't find you, so we went
back home. When we got home, there you were, sitting on our
porch. You support me: when I get a cut, you lick it. You cause
so much mischief. You have to wear diapers because you pee
all over the house. You are not a well-behaved dog, but I love
you still because you are sweet, funny, supportive, hyper, and
will eat everything you see, except for bread. I loved when you
stole my sister's sandwich, but didn't eat the bread. You are
the most awesome dog in the world. I love you so much. I have
always loved you and I always will.

Your best friend,
Sarah

Dear Ella,

The grace of vision in your right eye is gone, but the twinkle
still burns strong. In twelve years, you have seen much:
a farm built with you running behind the tractor, endless
days of veggies planted, weeding and more weeding. "Why,"
I know you ask, "do I ever weed so much?" Cold salmon days
swimming in Griffin Creek, Super Secret Swims, romps with
Flash and Sara J, two boys born, drives across the country,
Chautauqua LOVE, friends lost, battles with liver cancer;
every day we write a new chapter in gratitude. Your soothing
snore and one-of-a-kind swimming fragrance keep us real
and give us great vision! Vision and hope to smile and live
the days full. You fill my heart with infinite sweetness and
your paws pushing forward through the clear waters of the
chilled earth bring pure joy and the simple truth of how little
it really takes to be happy: a ball, a lake, a roll!

WE LOVE YOU, MISS ELLA!!!

Kathy Najimy: *Princess and Petie*

Dear Princess and Petie,

I have said this to your face many times and, every time I bare my soul, you stare at me blankly and refuse to respond. So I thought I'd write it in hopes of getting some kind of response from you. Maybe a little missive under my pillow? Or a sweet thank-you note? Sky-writing? Here is my letter:

I Love You. I Love You Individually, I Love You Together, and I Love You as a Species. IT IS NO SECRET THAT I PREFER DOGS TO MOST HUMANS. I say it every day to you, to my family, to pet-owning strangers, and on NBC talk shows. I love you for the same reasons that people who have been writing about dogs have been giving forever, so I won't give them again here. OK, maybe a couple. I love you because I never have to ask how your day was or tell you about mine. Because I never have to discuss square footage of your new apartment or ask what schools your kids are going to. I never have to lecture you about the virtue of rescuing dogs versus buying bred dogs, and I never have to remind you to VOTE.

It delights me we have similar tastes in TV shows and that you watch at the exact same times I do—and I love that we never, never have to comment on the downfall of civilization by reality TV. I love that I don't have to ask if you miss me when I am gone because when I return you are in the same position you were when I left and there is a pile of fur in the empty space where my suitcase was sitting before I left. I love that you look me in the eyes for a long, lovely time and I never ever once think, "Maybe I could use a breath mint or some eyeliner or Botox?" . . . ever.

I love you because you seem to me to be the most honest, deep, soulful beings on earth. Oh and you have very easy dietary requests, your dinner prep requires no knives, fennel, garlic peeling, or a particular kind of gluten-free almond milk. Thanks for that.

I love you.

Rosie O'Donnell: *Missy*

dear missy,

u arrived in my life just in time
my wounded heart needed some care
and there u were
snuggling close
always ready to give

u spent the first few weeks
in between my breasts
tucked in my sports bra
blond head sticking out
4 all 2 c

u survived the addition of roxy
ur new spunky sister
who outweighs u by half
yet u hold ur own
bossing her around

thanks for the love
the consistency
the tenderness

i love u

ps do u think u could work on using the wee wee pad?
i know it's a big house
but the rug under the coffee table
has been cleaned 40 times
come on kid—u can do it.

To my dear Mr. Pickle, better known as
My Little Man, or My One and Only Man,

I love and adore you from the bottom of my heart.
Thank you for putting up with my long work hours
   and my traveling.
Thank you God for setting Pickle in that window on the
   corner of 8th Avenue and 14th Street in the summer
   of 2009.
Now my life is complete. Tatum has Pickle and Pickle
   has Tatum. A love story.

The end.

Ken Paves: *Afton, Tajan, Honoree, and Jedah*

To my angels, my babies, my kiddos, the loves of
my life: Afton, Tajan, Honoree, and Jedah,

Afton, my oldest son and wild man, our protector but still
such a daddy's boy; my dearest Tajan, my white knight,
my gentle angel, my silly, silly cutie boy; Honoree, my
"womans," my beautiful, wild and crazy, funny girl who
loves her daddy so much; and Jedah, woman, prancy in all
your glory, so sweet and shy and full of love—my children,
I love you more than words could ever explain!

You have given me life, each of you has loved me, made
me laugh, and made me smile; you have been true best
friends—you are so much more; you are my family!

Each of you little angels were sent from God; I am
so grateful!

My beautiful children,
Daddy loves you!

Tyler Perry: *Aldo*

When I come home and the four of you come running
up to me, not knowing if I had a rough day or a good day,
you come in love.

If it was a rough day at work and I'm stressed, by the
time I walk into the house and get your treats for you, see
you jumping up and down so happy to see me, and see you
playing with each other, I literally feel the stress leaving me.

By the time we've taken a walk and played around in the
yard, I feel like I have more to give the world. You four do
that for me.

The humans that work for me would give you all medals,
if only they knew that if I didn't have the four of you their
lives would be much harder.

You give unconditional love and protection.

Who needs people . . . ? I've got you.

Thank you Peter, Paul, Mary, and Aldo
You make my life better.

Tyler Perry:
Peter, Mary, and Paul

Lulu Powers: *Mister Pickles and Teddy Kennedy*

Dear Mister Pickles,

My little buddy and my bodyguard. The way you look at me with the love in your eyes . . . "the mommy" stare, Stevie calls it. I get up, you get up. I drink my coffee and so do you. That has got to stop. I stay up late working—you are right there with me. You are just a precious bundle of love, who I love so much that, when I leave you and Teddy for more than a week, my heart aches for you. It truly hurts. I think you would be the boy giving me words of wisdom, where Teddy would tell me to "live, live, live." Just like Auntie Mame.

Mister Pickles, I have a vivid imagination but this would be a letter from you to me:

"Mom, I love you so much. You always take care of Teddy and me. Teddy acts a bit spoiled at times, he hogs everything, but as you said, he was on the streets and had to fend for himself. Is that why whenever you give us a bone, he wants mine and his? I usually just let him take it but I still do not understand why he growls at me when I walk by him. Then the next thing you know he gets one of his toys and wants me to play. Teddy should have been a baseball player or a high jumper. He throws his squirrel so far and we both run after it. I don't understand how he jumps so high. It must be nervous energy. I like when you say to your friends that I went to Harvard and Teddy went to Art Center. Mom, I do like your "sneekys" like you do. I even like your coffee, wine, and kefir. I am your best customer. I know I can be picky when I eat, but I only like homemade treats. I love when you make us eggs in the morning, put fish oil on them and say it is good for our skin. When Littia gives us a bath, I like the Jouer oil she puts on our coats. It makes me smell good and you seem to kiss me a lot more. Daddy and I have become close in the last couple years. Since my sister Sweetpea went to heaven. Oh, Teddy, stop it! I am not done yet . . ."

"Dear Mom—it's me, Teddy. Remember when I jumped into your arms at Mutts Rescue as you were on your way to the Larchmont Farmers Market? I heard you when you said, "I don't need another dog right now. I already have two." Well, that is when I started licking you more and nuzzling your neck. It worked. You told the lady to bring me over to see if I got along with your other dogs. Well, when we got to your house, I was so excited. I saw two new playmates. When Dad asked the rescue lady what they had been calling me, she answered "Teddy." Dad said, "He is our dog!" I am thankful that the rescuers started calling me Teddy because who knows where I would have ended up otherwise. It was meant to be. Is it true I was named after a senator? I heard you tell someone that when Senator Teddy Kennedy passed away, you wanted to honor him because he worked tirelessly in fighting for "the people" and you decided you were going to rescue a dog and name him Teddy Kennedy. I like that story. I am assuming that is why some of your friends call me "The Senator." That is what that Michael guy from New York City always calls me. Does Mister have a nickname like I do? I guess Senator Kennedy was kinda cool? So a couple of things. I love your cooking. I eat everything you give me, not like Mister, who is very picky. Mom, I do fake sleep when Mister wants to go to bed. Yes, I become deadweight and you have to pick me up like a baby . . . the paw trick works with you but not with Dad. I like to put my paw on your shoulder when you are in your bed so you know I am right next to you and you think I am cute. Sometimes it works, other times you put me to bed in my cage. I don't like the cage. Mister loves his . . . ."

Lulu

Dear Teddy,

You came along just like a song and brightened our day. You are crazy and we love you. You are continually making us laugh. You have no problem taking your dad's cigar and walking around with it or eating all the tomatoes from my garden. Nothing is off-limits to you. Well, Teddy, my other little buddy, thank you for coming along and bringing so much love to our lives.

Note: "God" spelled backward is "Dog". Need I say more?

Lulu

Kelly Preston: *Bear*

My dear, sweet Bear,

You found me when I needed you most. I looked in your
eyes and felt I'd known you before. I feel I know who
helped guide you to us. So fateful was that day along the
road where you were left.

   Your gentle sweetness helped heal my heart. Some say
we rescued you . . . I think it was the other way around.

Love, Kelly

Jill Rappaport: *Petey*

I is for IRRESISTIBLE because I cannot resist smothering you with hugs and kisses every time I see you.

L is for LANGUAGE, that special way we speak to each other.

O is for OBSESSED, which I proudly admit I am with you.

V is for VICTORY and I consider it a great one, that I rescued each one of you.

E is for EXPRESSION, your eyes and your one-of-a-kind faces that, with every head-tilt, melt my heart.

Y is for YOU; without you, my life would not be complete.

O is for OBVIOUS, which it is to my friends that I love my animals more than I do people. (Is that really such a bad thing?)

U is for UNCONDITIONAL and the UNBELIEVABLE love we have for one another!

Love, your Mommy

Dear KJ,

Can't imagine my life without you and I don't
wanna! You helped me beat cancer—licking my bald
head and laying your sweet head on whatever was
hurting me.
    How did you know?
    I love you!

Love,

Robin

Amy Rosenthal: *Cougar*

Dear Cougar,

Here's what happened one particular Thursday eight years ago. Our babysitter Emily stopped at the gas station on her way to our house. There she encountered the sad scenario of a drug addict trying to sell your stolen puppy self for a few quick bucks. Emily and her heart-of-gold of course came to your rescue. When she walked in the door, she told me what had happened, and that you were in her car just down the street (windows cracked open!) and that she was going to take you to the animal shelter after work. I wish I could tell you that I replied, "Go grab that poor little creature and bring him inside this instant!" But while sleeping dogs can lie, I can't. What I said was, "Whatever you do, Emily, please do not bring that dog anywhere near this house or near the kids." I'm so sorry, Cougar. But Justin, Miles, and Paris were eleven, nine, and seven and had been begging for a dog for roughly eleven, nine, and seven years each. Depending on my mood, my response was either: (a) No, never. You know I don't like dogs; (b) No, never. I will not be responsible for another living thing; or (c) No, never. I don't even want a plant. Good night.

A couple of hours later, the kids were all home from school. Justin had a neighborhood dog-walking job, so he set off on his usual route around the block. I went into my backyard studio to do some writing. If I were an accountant instead of a writer, perhaps I'd have done a better job of putting two and two together. A few minutes later, Justin comes running through the front door screaming, "Emily! Emily! There's a puppy in your car! Do you know there's a puppy in your car?! Miles, Paris! Emily has a puppy in her car!"

At this point, it was Me vs. Fate. I put up a really good case and won. But when I went out of town the next day, your father fell crazy in love with you, and the case was appealed and overturned. That was the first and last time I came home unhappy to see you. Thank you, Cougar, for somehow making your way to us . . . thank you for your patience with me those first days . . . thank you for the insane amount of joy you bring to our family . . . thank you for remaining so sweet and humble even though everyone who meets you falls in love with you because, let's face it, you're pretty much the best dog in the world. I love you so much, Cougie! Now when I come home, I'm more than just happy to see you. When I see you, it means I'm home.

Love and kisses forever and ever, Amy

To my lead dog, Breeze,

As we left the safety of the Grayling Iditarod checkpoint in 2009, I was aware of
the risk we were taking. We had opted to stay at the checkpoint the previous night
rather than venture out into what we were told was the worst weather the Yukon
had seen in over twenty years. The temperature was fairly cold, minus twenty
degrees Fahrenheit, but there was a fifty-mile-an-hour sustained headwind. I didn't
bother calculating how cold it really was because I didn't want to know. I knew that
the teams already making the run to Eagle Island, a run that should take roughly
seven hours, were taking fourteen hours. My race partner, Tim Osmar, and I had
decided to wait the storm out and leave in the morning, the idea being that the
storm would die down as the day progressed and our run to Eagle Island would be
easy. Tim knew of a shelter cabin halfway between the checkpoints where we could
stay if the storm did not abate as hoped. So, although going out into the storm was
a risk, we had trained for this for the last two years; many races have been won and
lost by people who took chances like this and I felt this was my opportunity to move
up in the field. Even though we were going into this storm on the same sixty-five-
mile stretch on which I had scratched in 2005, I knew we would make it because I
had you, my most confident lead dog, with me and the right team to go with you.

   Contrary to what we had been told, however, the storm did not calm down in the
afternoon and we walked through it all day. In the evening when Tim couldn't find
the cabin, we knew we couldn't go on, so we bedded down and I brought you into
my sleeping bag to keep me warm. I slept as well as could be expected that night,
made it to Eagle Island the next day, and went on to finish the race.

As I huddled close to you that night, I was reminded of another time when your bravery had saved my life: we had a film crew following us through the Dalzell Gorge in a helicopter and were having a rough run. The sound of the helicopter hovering directly over my head made it even worse and I couldn't imagine how you were able to focus and lead us through such a technical course with that incessant droning. But, as I looked forward, forcing myself to concentrate on my team and on the trail, there you were, with your cute little ears perked straight up, weaving through trees, and dodging holes in the ice. Then the helicopter engine began to sputter and I looked up to see it spinning toward the wall of the gorge. My eyes followed it down for a few seconds before I realized the potential danger we were in. Not knowing if the helicopter was going to fall straight down on top of us or crash into the wall of the gorge, raining debris down onto the trail, all I wanted was to get out of the way. "OK, get up!" I shouted. Whether you sensed the tension in my voice or were just excited to go faster, I will never know. But you motivated the team to run forward and the helicopter crash-landed in the spot where we had stood only seconds before.

It saddens me a little to know that your best racing years are behind you, but I am filled with great joy that you are still one of my best tour leaders. I never get tired of telling my guests how wonderful you are and of pointing out all your beautiful puppies who are following in your paw tracks. I'm full of hopeful anticipation as you and I watch them grow into the fine race dogs that we know they will become, and I will always remember the fine example you have set for them. Thanks for being the most adorable, sassiest bitch I have ever had. I love you.

Rachael

Dear Maggie,

You may know I don't enjoy your breath in my face when I'm sleeping, or you stepping on my feet when I'm putting on socks in the morning after you awaken me with dog breath and mournful moaning, but you are the dearest dog I've ever known. Yours is the best dog behavior ever!

Love,
Pop

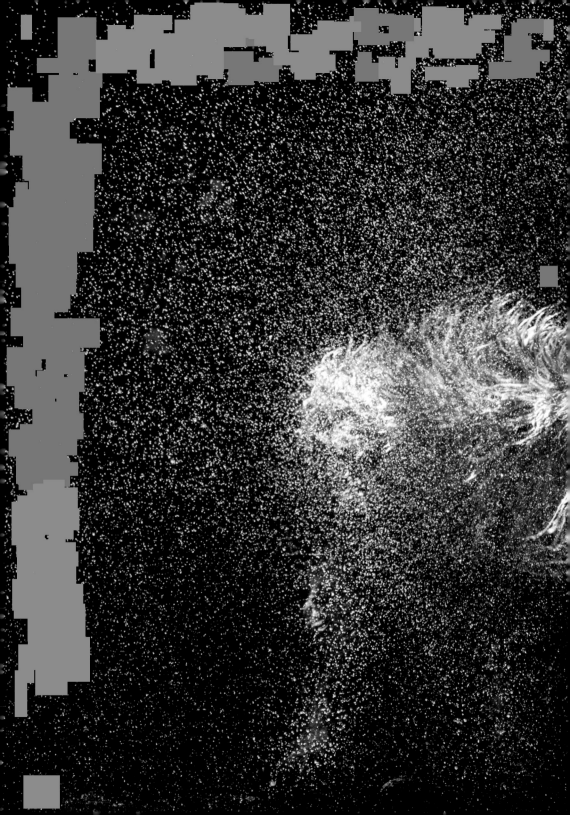

Oscar,

My sweet, sweet love . . .
I fell in love the moment I met you, so tiny and full
of puppy breath. You've been described as having
"Beverly Hills looks with a Compton attitude."
Seeing how happy you are swimming or running around
at the park are simple moments I cherish most!

I love you with all my heart!

Dear Abby,

I love you so much; you're so sweet and friendly!
I just don't like it when you pee everywhere!! :)
I love you!

Mommy

Dearest Ripley,

My littlest hero . . . it's hard to find the words to tell you just what you've meant to me over the last seven years. You came into my life at a time when I could barely take care of myself. I was in so much pain and was so, so lost. But I instantly fell in love with you, this tiny little creature running around the house looking like a baby deer. You were in a bad living situation and I had to help save you from the moment I saw you.

   But I was badly off myself. Most days I wouldn't have gotten out of bed except that you needed to be walked and fed. I remember those first few weeks together: if I wasn't in bed with you, I needed to be constantly moving. You and I crossed mile after mile, watching Christmas decorations be replaced with Valentine's decorations, then Easter decorations, then Fourth of July . . . and not only did you never once complain, you actually became excited when you heard the familiar jingle of your collar tags. Always up for an adventure!

I needed you so much those first few years that I couldn't bear to not have you with me everywhere I went. We became stealthy at sneaking you into various places . . . we even went to a movie together once. It makes me laugh to remember and I know you've long forgotten the smell of that popcorn. But you looked around for awhile, then snuggled in under my sweatshirt and no one was the wiser. You were so content to be my constant companion, always cuddled next to me in my darkest hours, always ready to go where I needed you to go. I honestly believe you saved my life, just as I believe I might have saved yours.

When you became sick, my depression lifted and I fought as hard as I could for both of us to make it through. It stopped being about what you were doing for me and became who I needed to be for you. You helped me grow up and focus on the world outside my head. You helped me want to get out of bed and experience life again . . . with you by my side of course!

Now that we're both older and wiser, we've settled into a pretty beautiful life together. You still jump around like a puppy when you hear your collar tags jingle, but you're also happy to snuggle down into a soft blanket on my lap. And you do a great job of not pestering the cats, by the way!

Every day is a joy, with your greetings when I get home from wherever I've been. You make me laugh with your mischievous spirit and my heart bursts with love every time you lay your sweet head on my chest for a cuddle. We still struggle with your health but I will trudge to the end of the earth to continue to be able to afford the medicine you need. Just as you trudged to the end of the earth to help heal me! You are the greatest gift I've yet been given in this life and I can't wait to see where we go next!

My love to you, sweet boy!

Min Pin Extraordinaire

Dear Cymbi,

I am writing to you today for a couple of reasons. I want to tell you how you came to be my dog, and I want to tell you why and how much I appreciate the important message you bring to me each day.

I always knew I wanted a dog once I retired from competition and could stay at home. When I began looking for my ideal dog, I knew that I needed a dog with a scary image, but I did not want a mean dog. I learned a few techniques for establishing which puppies in a litter are dominant and which are docile. Eventually, once I had decided on a pit bull, I visited a breeder on the West Coast. There I met your parents, Chase and Pearl. Together they displayed all the special traits I wanted in my dog: they were gentle, lovable, and friendly. So, I waited for the next litter. Five years later, nine puppies were born to Chase and Pearl. When I went to meet them, I planned to choose a puppy using the techniques I had learned for identifying docility. But, as dog owners well know, a dog often chooses you. And that is exactly what happened. This beautiful little reddish-brown puppy that looked like she was wearing mascara came up to me with a sweet little moaning greeting, as if to say "Hello." Then, she licked me and put her head between my ankles. That was that! I fell in love.

Today, you still greet me as you did that very first day, and I love the feeling. Cymbi, you are the dog of my dreams. You are obedient, friendly, and lovable. But more importantly, you are passive. That is perfect. You have a scary image, which makes you unapproachable to strangers. But you are a calm, submissive dog. You protect and tolerate my children's antics. You love me and them unconditionally. You give me a reason to love you, one of God's most faithful creatures, Man's Best Friend, my dog. You inspire me to try to "Be the person my dog thinks I am." I thank you for that, Cymbi.

Good dog! I love you, my Smunchy.

Dear Jack,

Thank you for being the perfect first pet. In May 1999,
after weeks of reading the paper and searching in NYC,
your dad and I said, "If they have a long-haired Jack Russell,
we're executing." Little did we know, it was to be our
lucky day. We knew as soon as we laid eyes on you in that
cage that we had to take you home.

   You were my first baby and you brought us so much joy.
After moving with us across the country a year later, you
kept me company during many lonely nights and protected
me when Dad was busy traveling. Sometimes you were
a little too protective, but it's all good. We wanted you to
have a friend, so Dad added another terrier (just what we
needed) to our growing family. Still protective, you took on
the big-brother role. Lucy acts as your sidekick and partner
in life, and we're thrilled you have each other.

   You've scared us a handful of times chasing your soccer
ball out in the middle of the San Francisco Bay—so far and
so determined that Dad had to go get you! You tested us
as we had to learn to give you shots twice a day. Having a
diabetic doggie has been a challenge, but it's amazing what
we can learn to do for someone out of love.

   Almost thirteen years later, you are still sleeping at
my feet every night and protecting me every day. I can't
imagine life without you and Lucy, so thank you for all you
have done. Our family is not complete without the joy
(and stinky farts) you bring to us all.

Xoxo, Mommy

Lisa Sugar: *Lucy*

Dear Sally and Sadie,

Thank you for being my personal alarm clocks every morning. Thank you for being my personal trainers . . . making sure I go for a walk outside every day. Thank you for being my bodyguards . . . barking at any small noises you hear.

I must admit, when I finally conceded to my son's begging for a dog, my rule was that there would be no pets in the house. Well, that lasted about a month . . . at the most. Now, I am the one who makes sure you are comfortable on the couch, with pillows under your heads. I am the one who backhands a raccoon, and tears my shoulder up, to make sure you all do not get attacked. When my mother comes to visit, even she cannot help but scoot over in bed to make room for you. Obviously, the tables have turned.

You get the front seat on all our boat rides and road trips to the beach. You entertain me as you jump off the diving board and climb the ladder in our pool. You make sure we don't have to eat leftovers by cleaning up what's left of dinner.

I never imagined I would sleep with a dog, much less two of you, but you all never fail to keep me warm at night. I never imagined how much I would look forward to being met at the door every single night by your smiling faces. You never fail to show me your love.

I never imagined I could love a dog the way

I love the two of you!

Kristen Timko: *Scruffy*

Dear Scruffy,

I wish we could talk with each other. If you could understand English (or if I could bark properly), I'd have so many questions for you and so many things I'd want you to know. Instead, all I can do is write this letter and make bad jokes about whether you had a "ruff" day.

When we brought you home from The Humane Society in June 2010, you were ten years old and in need of a lot of love. You hadn't been treated kindly before the shelter took you in and you were very sad. I wanted to take care of you and prove to you that you are a good boy. I felt like you deserved a good retirement home, as I like to call it. I've loved watching you grow over the last year and a half. You're eleven now but somehow you look younger than when we first met. I don't think you'd ever had a belly rub (because what dog doesn't roll over for one right away?) but now you love them, albeit while lying on your side. You still aren't sure how to play but you love your walks, and even on the days when we walk really, really slowly and get lapped by elderly people, I still love taking you on them. You're a really picky eater but the way you wag your tail when you know I've bought you a roasted chicken from the grocery store or when you know you're about to get one of your favorite treats makes me smile. You don't know, "sit," "stay," or any other commands, but I don't care. You're kind of like a honey badger that way—you do what you want—though you're much cuter and more cuddly. My husband—your doggy daddy—was initially very apprehensive about having a dog but now you're his little teddy bear and you even like him a little more than you like me. (I'll admit . . . that part stings a little!) Some people laud their dogs for their loyalty, their playfulness, and other qualities that make them Man's Best Friend. These dogs work hard for human affection. The tables are turned for us, but that's OK. I'll always be here for you, working to help you regain your trust in people and showing you what it's liked to be loved. If you never learn to give kisses, that's OK, too. Just promise me you know you're loved.

Love, Kristen

Dearest Louie and Manny,

I love you so much. Thank you for healing my heart.
And for letting me pick up your poo!

Love forever from,
That lady

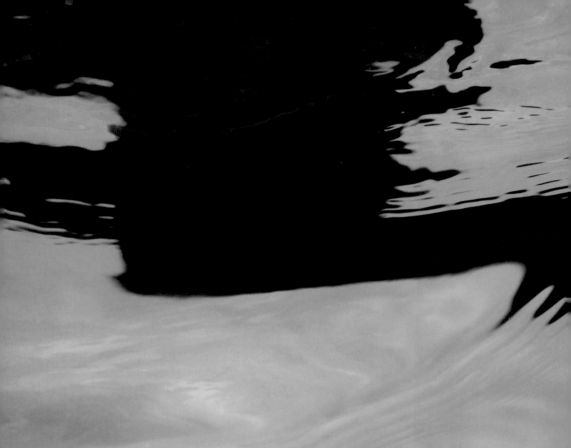

Dear Millie a.k.a. DaMoosers, Moose McGillicutty,
and Mrs. Velvet-ears,

This might seem a little odd because you can't read, so I'll explain it to you over a
beer and a few* treats very soon. I intended to write a letter thanking you for your
unconditional love and unwavering loyalty, qualities most dog lovers would agree
are the most beautiful you possess.

But instead, and I've given this a lot of thought, I'm writing to thank you for
letting ME love YOU! For letting me love you unconditionally, completely, with all
my heart, with no shame or fear, and with total childlike abandon, the "I'm glad the
guys on the hockey team can't hear me right now" kind of abandon.

I mean c'mon, some of the voices I use and things I say to you when we cuddle
would send any other woman—a less confident or understanding woman—

Michael Vartan: *Millie*

running for the hills, but not you. With your head on my lap, your incredible smile, you gaze at me with those deep-brown eyes and exhale the most contented groan. In those moments, those splendid little moments, all is well in the world; it really is.

You are the most gentle and tender creature I know: your sweet little essence ever soothing to my soul. With you, I can be weak, I can be insecure, completely flawed and utterly useless, yet you love me all the same, never criticizing or passing judgment (which is really cool, 'cause more times than not I'm all those things!).

So, in closing, thank you for being my best friend, my faithful companion, and above all else, my dog! Oh, and also for having the softest ears in the universe, literally, in the entire universe, all of it, the softest!

All my love, your wildest admirer and faithful companion. Dad.

* "few" in our household means a Labrador's dozen

Rumer Willis: *Harlow, Zhuz, and Sadie*

My three girls, my life wouldn't be the same without you. I can't imagine how we found each other, but I thank the universe every day for putting you in my life. I hope that as we all grow and age, I can share with you everything I have to offer and more. I hope I can give you everything you could ever want or need, and that your lives will be more than you ever imagined. I love you my baby girls.

All my love,
Momma

Zhuz,
My teeny little white bat. I loved you from the moment I saw you. I felt such a need to take you and protect you from all the world. You were so scared and shy, and you have blossomed into such an outgoing little monkey. You have all at once the ability to be a crazy little monster and to be the sweetest munchkin that I can't resist. You are insanely codependent, and while some might shun away from this, I could not love you more for it. You are the best snuggler, and when you curl up on my chest, fall asleep, and rest your head on my cheek, I swear sometimes I wonder how I found such a light. I love you so much, little bean.

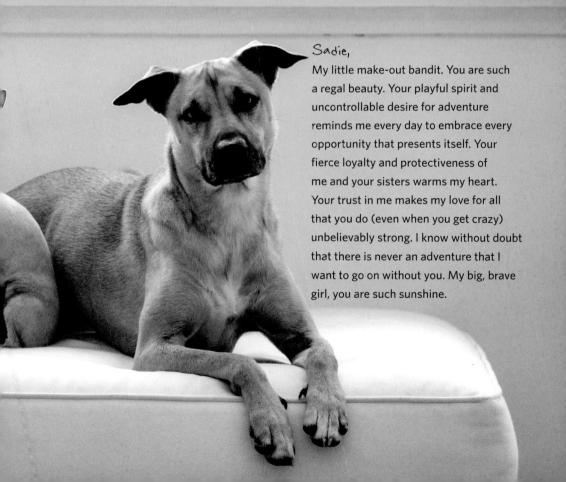

Harlow,

My little mama. You were the first to come in and drive me absolutely bonkers. You were such a tiny little thing, but you have turned out to be such an important part of my life. We have traveled the world, you and me. You have been such a trooper wherever we went. You lead the pack, my sweet. When you were attacked by the coyote, I thought I was going to die . . . be absolutely devastated, but you are so strong and you're such a fighter. I don't think I've ever been so happy to see your little smiling face.

Sadie,

My little make-out bandit. You are such a regal beauty. Your playful spirit and uncontrollable desire for adventure reminds me every day to embrace every opportunity that presents itself. Your fierce loyalty and protectiveness of me and your sisters warms my heart. Your trust in me makes my love for all that you do (even when you get crazy) unbelievably strong. I know without doubt that there is never an adventure that I want to go on without you. My big, brave girl, you are such sunshine.

Oprah Winfrey: *Luke (a.k.a. Wonder Boy)*

My handsome Wonder Boy,

Every time I look into your eyes, I can see all the way to the marrow of your heart.

I quite simply adore you. And love that you can't seem to get enough love from anyone. You're always pawing for more. More hugs, more rubs, more kisses on your gorgeous muzzle.

From the first day we took you home, there was a majesty about you. You were the regal one with depth and soul. You were supposed to be Stedman's dog. But for sure, your heart belongs to me. And mine to you. When all the others are out busy sniffing for adventure, you're the one who returns repeatedly to the trail to see if I'm OK and following your lead, the one waiting on the porch for my return from places too far off for a dog mind to ponder.

You're in the now, always present. Always Love. You're my Alpha.

You're my dear, handsome Wonder Boy.

Dear Sadie a.k.a. Sadie Mae (what Stedman calls you),
Sadie Lady, Gorgeous Girl, Farrah Fawcett,

On a cold, windy Sunday morning, with banks of snow layering the sidewalks, Stedman and I bundled ourselves up for a return trip to PAWS (a no-kill shelter in Chicago). I had spotted you there the day before, and couldn't stop thinking about you. It was definitely puppy love at first sight.

Our first night together sealed our deal forever. Against my better judgment I acquiesced to your crying, took you out of the crate, and put you in bed with me. After a restless night, not wanting to hurt your tiny eight-week-old self, I awakened to find you sleeping on top of my head. You treated me like a mama litter-buddy, with your wet little nose pressed inside my ear.

Since then we've spent a lot of nights snuggling, sharing secrets of our hearts.

I've tossed a lot of balls and watched you catch them midair, then wag your whole body in delight with your accomplishment.

Wherever I am, you are. In the kitchen, in the tub, on the phone, you can track me.

You're the one who gets to travel to different cities, hotels, backstage events, and the office every day. You've seen a lot of the world yet maintained a sweetness about you, with all your body-wagging confidence and self-esteem.

Stedman tells you all the time that "you're special"; I'm sure you already know it.

Love you, girl.

Luci Woodley: *Sis*

Dear Sis,

These things I know:

I know you stole my peanuts, because your breath smelled like the roasted Virginia legumes I left on the table.

I know you broke into the birdseed and picked out all the sunflower seeds, because I saw the cracked shells in your gums.

I know you were on my desk, standing on my laptop, because I saw the gibberish you typed.

I know you spend the day in downward-dog tonguing food pellets out of your Pet Bistro.

I know you shriek in my ear when visitors approach because you believe an early warning system is the best.

I know I find myself on the edge of the bed because you believe horizontal is the best way to sleep.

I forgive you for all these infractions, Sis, because you are a special being: you are a thinker. You stop and analyze situations. You pick up a routine in a split second. You can tell time and know how to count. You are supremely intelligent, thoughtful, curious, and, yes, kind.

You opened my eyes to not just your world, but the entire animal kingdom. From the creepy crawlers to the largest species on Earth, because of you I know that animals are so much more intelligent and complex than we give them credit for. I don't run screaming from the spiders, and the snakes, and the lizards, and the rats because I stop and see how their lives matter. This knowledge has enriched me to become a more understanding and compassionate human being, and this radiates out to care about all living things.

Your presence on this earth is so much more than about you and me. It's about all of us, humans and animals.

Thank you for that, Sis.

Meet the family . . .

Kristin Chenoweth: *Maddie*

Rory Barish and Nike Rory Barish's beloved dog Nike (16) sadly passed on November 23, 2011. She was adopted from German Shepherd Rescue in Los Angeles and courageously battled injuries and traumas throughout her life. Nike was Rory's soulmate and the most loyal companion, spending days on Manhattan Beach making friends with the locals. Rory is a high-end real estate agent in Beverly Hills, a motivational speaker, competitive swimmer, and former model. Two weeks after Robin took these photographs, Nike peacefully passed away in her owner's arms at their favorite spot on the beach.

Martha Beck and Bjorn Martha Beck is a life coach, bestselling author, and O, *The Oprah Magazine* columnist. She and her family are the devoted owners of Bjorn (9), a large, proud, but secretly somewhat cowardly golden retriever, who rules the roost.

Tony Bennett and Happy Happy Benedetto, a 4-year-old Maltese, is happy as Larry being the beloved pooch of music legend Tony Bennett and his wife, Susan Benedetto. Happy accompanies Tony on many outings around Manhattan. Tony has won no less than seventeen Grammy Awards and is also a painter. Susan has been a teacher and administrator in art high schools. Together they founded Exploring the Arts, a nonprofit organization that supports and funds arts education in public schools.

Whitney Biggs and Zoe When Whitney Biggs was suffering from breast cancer, her sister suggested that pet therapy would be healing for her and her family. Zoe came to them from the North Pole, via Santa himself, wrapped in a big red bow! Whitney says Zoe became the best medicine for all kinds of ailments, from skinned knees to her cancer. She lives in Tennessee with her husband and their two children.

Nicole Brown and Dorothy Nicole Brown adopted Dorothy (5) from United Yorkie Rescue after Dorothy was severely injured by her previous owners' children. Nicole was asked to see if she could rehabilitate Dorothy by using water therapy to help her heal physically and emotionally. Dorothy's quality of life was so poor that euthanasia seemed the only alternative. Fortunately, she adapted very quickly to her new life on wheels, and in the process won Nicole's heart. Dorothy has since become a therapy dog and brings joy to all who meet her. Nicole owns Miami Pet Concierge, a pet care company based in Miami, Florida, and also lives with Gus, a rescued terrier mix, and her cat, Elle.

Adam Browning and Stanley Adam Browning and his wife named their Labrador, Stanley, after the town in Idaho where they were married. Stanley (7) usually accompanies Adam when he walks his twins. Max and Lilly, to preschool. Stanley makes a lot of friends on the route; Adam is pretty sure everyone knows Stanley's name but not his.

Colbie Caillat, Maté, and Plummy Maté (1) was found at a rescue in Orange County by singer-songwriter Colbie Caillat. He's a crossbreed of miniature pinscher, Shih Tzu, Papillon, and Australian shepherd. Colbie also adopted Plum (around 5–7) from the Southern California Golden Retriever Rescue, who was part of a group of abused dogs rescued from the streets of Taiwan. Colbie is a two-time Grammy Award–winning artist whose three albums have sold over seven million copies worldwide. She has performed at the White House and the Nobel Peace Prize Concert. She is active in the Surfrider Foundation, Farm Sanctuary, Save the Music, and The Humane Society of the United States, for whom she was the spokesperson for Puppy Mill Action Week.

Kim Carney and Pixel Three-year-old Pixel was rescued from Lil' Waif Puppy Rescue by graphic designer and illustrator Kim Carney. She couldn't resist Pixel's Chihuahua mix. Kim and her husband have more than three animals at home, which is apparently against city regulations; Kim's husband worries that she could become a dog hoarder later in life.

Casa Pacifica and Archie Casa Pacifica Centers for Children and Families help abused and neglected children and adolescents and assist them in overcoming some of life's most difficult circumstances. Archibald Razz-M-Tazz, "Archie" (7) was donated to Casa Pacifica Centers for Children and Families after research showed that the Newfoundland breed is one of the best to work with troubled and abused youth. Archie comforts scared children when they first arrive at Casa Pacifica, offering his fluffy coat for them to cry into and his big body for them to hug. He loves to play soccer with them and is a patient listener and friend to all. www.casapacifica.org.

Kristin Chenoweth and Maddie Kristin Chenoweth named her Maltese after one of her favorite actresses, Madeline Kahn. Maddie (8) has been with Kristin on her Broadway, TV, and movie sets and has met all of her boyfriends! Kristin says, "She is my child with fur. She doesn't really like my singing voice though. She leaves the room when I rehearse and I try to tell her that audiences pay to 'hear mommy sing,' but she just doesn't care." Kristin is an Emmy and Tony Award–winning singer and actress.

Cat Cora and Harlow Chef, author, and mother of four boys, Cat Cora has become one of the largest names in the culinary community since becoming the first and only female Iron Chef on *Iron Chef America* in 2005. She and her family rescued Harlow (3), a Chihuahua, an experience that Cat believes is incredibly rewarding both for owners and pets.

Megan DeWeerdt and Mokie Megan DeWeerdt, a stay-at-home-mom from San Francisco, needed a special dog for her home—one that was completely trustworthy around children, house-trained, and didn't mind cats. Mokie (9) was adopted from Golden Gate Lab Rescue League two years ago when her previous owner had to move house and couldn't take Mokie with her. She had raised Mokie with such tender loving care that Mokie was a settled and calm presence in Megan's family.

Fran Drescher and Esther Actress, producer, and activist Fran Drescher became internationally famous for her TV sitcom *The Nanny*, which also starred her first Pomeranian, Chester. When Chester passed at the age of 18, Fran was heartbroken, but then Esther came into her life to teach her that "there is love after love." Esther (11) is the newest cast member of Fran's series *Happily Divorced*. A uterine cancer survivor, Fran is the president and founder of the Cancer Schmancer Movement dedicated to early detection and prevention. She has authored two bestsellers and a children's book and continues to advocate civil liberties and be a public diplomacy envoy for women's health issues.

Fran Drescher: *Esther*

Christine Grant: *Stormy*

Ethan Duck (right) with Owen Duck and Sammy The Duck family adopted their golden retriever when he was five months old. Sammy's first owner was in the military but couldn't take Sammy with him when he was assigned to a new base. Now eighteen months old, Sammy is a constant buddy to 9-year-old Ethan Duck and his 4-year-old brother, Owen. When Owen was born, the nurse asked Ethan what his new brother's name was. Ethan replied: "Samson Bonecrusher Duck." Although the name didn't suit his new little brother, it was a perfect fit for their loving, gentle golden retriever who can destroy a bone in just a matter of minutes. The boys love wrestling, and Sammy does, too!

Hilary Duff and DuBois Singer, actress, and entrepreneur Hilary Duff and her NHL hockey veteran husband, Mike Comrie from the Pittsburgh Penguins, have four dogs—Jak, a terrier; two Chihuahuas, Coco and Lola; and five-year-old DuBois, a Bernese mountain dog/ Australian shepherd mix. DuBois was adopted from his foster parents who found him in South Bay, Los Angeles, living under a bush, malnourished, and neglected. Love and care has turned DuBois into a strong protector and solid leader of the Duff-Comrie pack.

Chet Frith and Gunner Chet Frith is a veteran of the Iraq war who acquired Gunner (2) to help him deal with posttraumatic stress disorder. Gunner is a golden retriever trained by Patriot Service Dogs of Florida, a nonprofit organization that raises and trains dogs to help those with disabilities—especially veterans. Gunner has made an overwhelmingly positive impact on Chet's life since he was gifted to him on Veteran's Day 2011.

Christine Grant and Stormy Christine Grant's dog was born during one of the rare snowstorms in Scottsdale, Arizona, so she was named Lolenda's Heart of the Storm, a.k.a. Stormy. When Christine met the litter as pups, Stormy was the first to pounce at her feet, and she's been a wonderful companion ever since. The 5-year-old Labrador retriever is also a very good hunting dog.

Chelsea Handler and Chunk Chelsea Handler adopted Chunk (10), a Chow-Chow/ German shepherd mix, from a shelter in 2009. Chunk had a reputation as a problem dog, but when a shelter worker took him under her wing, he developed into an affectionate, eager-to-please learner. Unfortunately, he was red-listed, but the volunteer initiated a campaign to save him on social networking sites and in the media, and at the eleventh hour, Chunk was rescued. Comedian Chelsea is the host of the hit late-night comedy show *Chelsea Lately* and a bestselling author.

Jackie Hassine and Oliver Jackie Hassine was grieving for her recently passed Labrador, Jasper, when Oliver (4) came into her life unexpectedly. After being adopted, Oliver helped Jackie and her other dog, Max, to heal and brought them much joy. Now Max has also passed, but Oliver, an adorable mutt of unknown breed mix, continues to uplift the spirits of all around him. Jackie lives in Coconut Grove, Florida, and volunteers at Everglades Outpost wildlife sanctuary in her spare time.

Mariel Hemingway, Tree, and Bindu Bindu, an 11-year-old Yorkshire terrier, was adopted for actress Mariel Hemingway's daughter, Dree. Bindu travels the world with Mariel and has been on location all over the United States. Tree is a 3-year-old border collie who was rescued eighteen months ago; he had rarely been out of a crate. From being constantly terrified of people, Tree has transformed into a smart and sociable animal who melts everyone's hearts. Mariel is an Oscar and Golden Globe–nominated actress, writer, wellness spokesperson, and the creator of a support site for mental illness and suicide called You Matter, Don't Quit. Mariel also has a wellness website with her partner, Bobby Williams: www.thewillingway.com.

Barbra Horowitz and Buddha When Barbra Horowitz's sister adopted a pug, Barbra couldn't resist adopting his adorable brother. She named him Buddha, and he is now 13 years old. Called Hollywood's personal stylist by *People* magazine, Barbra has been dressing men and women of all sizes, ages, and incomes since 2004. She is a fashion writer, on-air personality, and the author of *Closet Control*.

Linda Israel and Tura Lu Linda Israel has had the pleasure of having Bernese mountain dogs in her life for over twenty-three years. Linda says Tura Lu is "10 years young." Inspired by her love of animals, Linda paints to express a deep connection to the beauty of the earth, the animal kingdom, and to share her joy of color with others.

Kirsten Kenny and Cooper Kirsten Kenny and her husband searched high and low for the perfect pup to extend their family and found the puggle, a cross between a beagle and a pug. They fell in love with Cooper (4) at first sight. With his squished face and bug eyes, they knew they just had to have him. Kirsten is a stay-at-home mother of a one-year-old daughter and lives in Chicago.

Emily Kraper and Palmer When Emily was young, her mother felt that her children needed a family-oriented, oversize lapdog with a spotted nose, and Molly, an English springer spaniel, joined the family. For seventeen years, Molly loyally ensured that her breed became irreplaceable for all members of the family. When Emily married, it was only a matter of time before she would ask for a springer puppy. Her husband John agreed, as long as he could give the dog a name inspired by Wake Forest University, and Palmer (1), named after golf legend and WFU alumnus Arnold Palmer, came to be.

Jennifer La Farge Perry and Bailey Mae Jennifer La Farge Perry gave Bailey Mae (now 4) to her daughter for her eighteenth birthday. Boston terriers are sometimes called "American gentlemen." Jennifer runs the nonprofit Children's Action Network in Los Angeles, which focuses on raising awareness about children in foster care who need adoptive families.

Cynthia McFadden: *Sparky*

Anna Mialky: *Crosby*

Carol Leifer and Albert Carol Leifer went to help a friend adopt a dog from their local shelter and couldn't resist adding Albert (4), a terrier mix, to her brood of six rescues. Carol is an Emmy-nominated writer and comedian whose thirty-year career includes writing for *Seinfeld* and *Saturday Night Live*; starring in four of her own comedy specials that have aired on HBO, Showtime, and Comedy Central; and penning the book *When You Lie about Your Age, the Terrorists Win*. Carol hopes that "one day we will live in a world where no dogs or cats are euthanized anymore. Adopt, don't shop!"

Hannah Lewis and Daphne Daphne (7) was adopted from the Rescue Rover Foundation in Redondo Beach, California, by Hannah Lewis. Daphne is a crossbreed of mastiff, boxer, and dachshund. Hannah is a dentist living in Laguna Beach but grew up in Palos Verdes, so considers both Daphne and herself to be "California Girls."

Armando Martinez and Roscoe First-grader Armando Martinez is the winner of the Chicago International Charter Schools—Bucktown *A Letter to My Dog* contest. At six years old, Armando is only two years older than his solid bullmastiff, Roscoe. Armando is an only child but Roscoe provides much fun and friendship. When he grows up Armando wants to be a watchmaker.

Cynthia McFadden and Sparky Sparky (7) has been the happy heart at the center of Cynthia McFadden's family for seven years, her son Spencer having begged for a dog since he first began to speak ("dog" was his second word!). Cynthia has been traveling the world reporting for ABC News for seventeen years. Her distinguished reporting has won many of broadcasting's most coveted awards including the Emmy, the Peabody, the duPont, and the Foreign Press Award. For the past six years she has been the coanchor of *Nightline*. McFadden has focused much of her investigative work on human rights abuses, particularly those faced by women and children.

Maria Menounos, Athena, and Apollo Journalist and actress Maria Menounos was doing a story for the *Today* show on the abuses of puppy mills when a poodle with sixty stitches up her spine gently placed her head onto Maria's lap. The dog had been beaten by the puppy mill owner. Maria and her boyfriend adopted her and named her Athena, which made a perfect match for their other dog, Apollo.

Anna Mialky and Crosby Nearly one hundred letters written by students at Granville Schools in Ohio were submitted in a contest for inclusion in this book. Anna Mialky's letter to Crosby Rose was chosen as one of the winners. Crosby was a surprise gift in a picnic basket from Anna's mom and dad. The 2-year-old golden retriever is much loved by Anna and her sisters, Clare and Emma. Anna is a fourth grader who enjoys figure skating, reading, swimming, visiting her grandparents in Pittsburgh, and playing with Crosby, of course.

Sarah Mortellaro and Sammy Sarah Mortellaro's letter to Sammy (4) was one of the winning entries in the *A Letter to My Dog* contest at Granville Schools in Ohio. Sarah and her two sisters begged their parents for a dog. They searched high and low for a nonshedding dog and finally found Sammy, a West Highland white terrier. Sarah wants to be a doctor one day, maybe a vet, and plans to own her own farm. She really wants a teacup pig as a companion for Sammy!

Wendy Munroe and Ella Wendy Munroe and Andrew Stout picked out Ella-Ellie-Lallie-Love-Girl from her litter in Grand Coulee, Washington. As a pup she had a howl like Ella Fitzgerald, so she was named after the singer. Wendy and Andrew began Full Circle Farm sixteen years ago and now have four hundred acres growing certified organic produce. Their Farm to Table program has over nine thousand members throughout Washington, Idaho, Alaska, and California. Ella (12) has been with them and their two boys every step of the way.

Kathy Najimy, Petie, and Princess Princess Steinem (9) and Petie Starbucks (4) were rescued by actress and activist Kathy Najimy. Princess is a corgi mix that the shelter said had "personality problems," but Kathy and her husband, actor/singer Dan Finnerty, were not deterred: "We ALL have personality problems," says Kathy. Petie, a Chihuahua mix, who had a frenetic energy at the rescue lady's house but thankfully calmed down at Kathy and Dan's. Kathy has appeared in over twenty-five films including *Sister Act* and *Hocus Pocus*, and several TV shows including *Veronica's Closet*, *King of the Hill*, *Numb3rs*, and *The Kathy and Mo Show*. She has starred on Broadway and has been named *Ms. Magazine* Woman of the Year and PETA Humanitarian of the Year.

Rosie O'Donnell and Missy Actress and comedienne Rosie O'Donnell found love and healing through Missy (4), her long-haired Chihuahua. Rosie's film and TV career spans twenty-five years. She has written two autobiographies and a craft book for kids.

Tatum O'Neal and Mr. Pickle Mr. Pickle (3) is a charming Maltese-Yorky and the man in Tatum O'Neal's life. Tatum is an actress and author whose career spans two decades and many media. She is best known as the youngest person ever to win an Oscar but considers her role as mother of three wonderful children her most important one.

Ken Paves, Afton, Taj, Honoree, and Jedah Celebrity hairstylist Ken Paves is so enamored with Salukis that he has a brood of four, from left: Afton Blake (9), Taj (7), Honoree (5), and Jedah (4). Each dog came into Ken's life at a serendipitous moment. Afton and Taj are his older boys, and Honoree and Jedah are "daddy's little girls," who truly live up to the Saluki characteristics of poise and presence; Salukis are also known as the royal dog of Egypt. Ken's numerous appearances on TV programs such as *The Oprah Winfrey Show*, *The Biggest Loser*, and *The X Factor* have made his hair makeovers and products world famous.

Tyler Perry, Aldo, Peter, Paul, and Mary Tyler Perry's inspirational journey from the hard streets of New Orleans to the heights of Hollywood's A-list as an actor, director, producer, songwriter, playwright, and more is the stuff of American legend. Tyler grew up in an impoverished household scarred by abuse; this experience gave him the strength, faith, and perseverance that form the foundations of his much-acclaimed plays films, books, and shows. He may be an extremely busy man, but he always has time for his dogs. He has said his first dog, Aldo (6), a German shepherd, became his "best buddy." And when Tyler visited his local humane society to adopt a pal for Aldo, he went home with three husky mixes! Peter, Paul (a girl), and Mary are all three years old.

Lulu Powers, Mr. Pickles, and Teddy Kennedy Lulu Powers adopted Teddy Kennedy (3) from a Mutts rescue, spotting him as she was on her way to the Larchmont Farmers' Market one Sunday. Lulu is a bestselling author and entertaining designer, celebrated for her accessible culinary creations and impeccable styling. Lulu and her husband, photographer Stephen Danelian, live in Los Angeles with Teddy and Mr. Pickles (6).

Lisa Sugar: *Jack and Lucy*

Robin Roberts: *KJ*

Kelly Preston and Bear Bear (3) was rescued by actress Kelly Preston and her family. They found him emaciated on the side of the road. Now Bear is a healthy and happy dog, who eats organic food. Kelly's notable films include *Jerry McGuire*, *For Love of the Game*, and *The Last Song*. She is a strong supporter of parents and children's rights, drug rehabilitation, education, and environmental issues. Kelly is a proud mother of three beautiful children, Jett, Ella Bleu, and Benjamin, and is married to international star John Travolta.

Jill Rappaport, Buckaroo, C.J., Sweet Pea, and Petey Jill Rappaport has seven horses and four rescue dogs: a yellow Labrador, Buckaroo (10-ish); an American bulldog, Petey (6-ish); a Havanese, C.J. (7-ish); and a coonhound mix, Sweet Pea (11-ish). She has worked on NBC's *Today* show for twenty-one years, beginning as entertainment correspondent, but later, when her beloved dog Jack developed bone cancer, she realized that animal welfare issues were her calling. Now, as animal advocate for *Today*, Jill has received numerous awards, including the coveted Genesis Award twice, the first Voice for the Animals Award from The Humane Society of the United States, the MSPCA-Angell's Animal Hall of Fame Award, and the 2012 Global Pet Expo's Excellence in Journalism and Outstanding Contributions to the Pet Industry Award. She was also named the American Society for the Prevention of Cruelty to Animals (ASPCA) Good Will Equine Welfare Ambassador and was given the honor of ringing the New York Stock Exchange Opening Bell for animal welfare. Rappaport is also a bestselling author of four books, including three about animals, and has created a leash and collar line to promote adoption, called the Jill Rappaport Rescued Me Collection, along with an equestrian jewelry line named Hannah's Heart, after her beloved mare, to benefit the ASPCA.

Robin Roberts and KJ Robin Roberts, *Good Morning America* anchor and author of *From the Heart: Seven Rules to Live By*, gave KJ (Killer Jack) as a gift to a dear friend. When her friend moved to Europe, Robin adopted the Jack Russell terrier, now 14. A college basketball star, Robin was inducted into the Women's Basketball Hall of Fame in 2012. Robin supports numerous causes including the fight against cancer; she herself is a breast cancer survivor.

Amy Rosenthal and Cougar Amy Krouse Rosenthal has been a writer for over one hundred years (that is, in dog years). She is a *New York Times* bestselling author of children's books and her memoir *Encyclopedia of an Ordinary Life* was named a top-ten memoir of the decade. She's a long-time contributor to Chicago Public Radio, YouTube, and the TED conferences. She lives online at whoisamy.com and for real in Chicago with her husband, children, and, of course, Cougar, a black Labrador-cross.

Rachael Scdoris and Breeze Rachael Scdoris is a professional sled-dog racer and endurance athlete. She lives outside Bend, Oregon, with her twenty-two dogs, all specially bred from Alaskan huskies, German shorthairs, English setters, or foxhounds to be incredibly athletic and friendly and have short hair. Rachael was born with congenital achromatopsia, making her legally blind. As a young girl, Rachael made the decision not to allow her impaired vision to stand in the way of her dreams and has been racing sled dogs since age 11. In 2006, she was the first legally blind racer to finish the Iditarod—the Super Bowl of sled-dog racing. Rachael has been formally honored by the Women's Sports Foundation, Oregon Commission for the Blind, Goodwill Industries, Foundation Fighting Blindness, National Association for Girls and Women in Sport, and Perkins School for the Blind, and has been nominated for an ESPN Excellence in Sports Performance Yearly Award and the prestigious Congressional Medal of Honor Society's Above and Beyond Citizen's Honor award. In 2002, Rachael was selected to carry the torch to the Winter Olympic Games in Salt Lake City.

Tom Skerritt and Maggie Mae Tom Skerritt's lovable Maggie Mae is an 8-year-old greater Swiss mountain dog, a working-breed dog with a wonderful disposition. Tom is best known for his roles in *M*A*S*H*, *Alien*, *Top Gun*, *A River Runs Through It*, and *Picket Fences*. He also performs in various local productions in Seattle and is cofounder of THEFILMSCHOOL, which teaches the art of story telling. Tom enjoys spending time in the beautiful Northwest with his family and friends and of course keeping the dish full of fish flakes for Zoey the cat.

Amy Smart and Oscar A friend of Amy Smart's went on a date with an actor who had been given Oscar as a gift and couldn't keep him. Amy came to the rescue and brought the soft-coated wheaten terrier home. Amy is a film and television actress and former model. She lives in California with her husband, Carter Oosterhouse, Oscar (8), Carter's bulldog Slim, and two cats. Amy helps out at organizations such as Best Friends Animal Society, Heal the Bay, Environment California, and the Environmental Media Association. She'd like to see more people adopting dogs from shelters instead of buying them.

Willow Smith and Abby At the age of 11, Willow Smith has already been seen on the big and small screens opposite some of today's most successful actors and actresses, including her father Will Smith. She is also a double-platinum recording artist and in September 2011 earned a place in the Guinness Book of World Records as youngest ever transatlantic top-twenty artist. Willow currently lives with her dog Abby (1), a Yorkshire terrier, and her family, in California.

Sarah Stanze and Ripley Ripley Merlin (9) once belonged to a couple but the husband didn't like him. This was inconceivable to Sarah Stanze, who gladly gave the miniature pinscher a new, loving home. Sarah says she's so lucky to live in Portland, Oregon, where there are countless opportunities to be outside and enjoy nature with her sidekick Ripley.

Picabo Street and Cymbi Alpine ski racer Picabo Street was the first American woman to win the World Cup International Championship in the Downhill two years in a row. She won gold medals in the Super Giant Slalom at the 1998 Winter Olympics and in the Downhill at the 1996 World Championships. Picabo was inducted into the US Ski and Snowboard Hall of Fame in 2004 and the US Olympic Hall of Fame in 2009. Picabo enjoys spending time with her four children and of course, her dog Amber Lite Chase Me Cymbidium a.k.a. Cymbi (8), an American Staffordshire terrier. Picabo works with several humanitarian groups including the Picabo's Street of Dreams Foundation, which she founded to help people chase their dreams.

Lisa Sugar, Jack, and Lucy Online media entrepreneurs Lisa and Brian Sugar had already adopted four kittens from shelters but had always talked about getting a dog as well. Jack, a Jack Russell mix, appeared in their lives the week of Brian's birthday—the perfect present. The Sugar family now comprises two daughters, Katie and Juliet, and two Jack Russells, Jack (13) and Lucy (11).

Rumer Willis: *Sadie*

Oprah Winfrey: *Luke*

Pat Summitt, Sally (left), and Sadie (right) Sally (10) and Sadie Summitt (4) are mother and daughter Labrador retrievers. They are beloved dogs of Pat Summitt, head coach of the University of Tennessee Lady Volunteer basketball team, and the coach with the most wins in NCAA basketball history. In 2011, Pat bravely revealed that she had been diagnosed with early onset dementia, Alzheimer's type, and through The Pat Summitt Foundation is working to raise funds to promote education, provide support, and encourage research into the disease.

Kristen Timko and Scruffy Kristen Timko met Scruffy (11), a Shih Tzu mix, on her first day as a volunteer at the local humane society: she looked after him during an adoption event and a lot of people thought he was her dog. She instantly knew Scruffy was meant to be part of her life, but it took a few weeks to convince her husband. Eventually he agreed, and Scruffy joined their little family, where he has been spoiled and loved ever since.

Nia Vardalos, Manny, and Louie Nia Vardalos, the actress and writer of *My Big Fat Greek Wedding*, and her husband, actor Ian Gomez, adopted Manny (8), a Labrador retriever, from Pet Finder six years ago. Louie (2) was found on the street ten months before this photo was taken. His ear was bitten through and he had chewed off a rope tied around his neck. When no one claimed him, he was adopted into the family and their daughter named him Louie Salvatore Dominick Bagel Vardalos Gomez.

Michael Vartan and Millie French-American actor Michael Vartan is passionate about animal causes and engages in helping raise funds, promoting awareness, and protecting animals of all species around the world. A friend in Colorado sent Michael a photo of the runt of his litter and Millie the chocolate Labrador was adopted immediately. Michael appears on the PETA website with Millie (8) sharing his dog-care tips. Michael has starred in television and in film, coming to international acclaim with his starring role as Agent Michael Vaughn on the worldwide hit ABC series *Alias*. In his limited free time, Vartan feeds his obsession with sports, particularly ice hockey.

Rumer Willis, Harlow, Zhuz, and Sadie The oldest daughter of Demi Moore and Bruce Willis, Rumer Willis is a big animal lover. Her "beautiful babies" are Sadie (4) a German shepherd mix, and Chihuahuas Harlow (5) and Zhu Zhu (1). Harlow was found when Rumer was shooting a movie in Pittsburgh, and Sadie came from the Pasadena Humane Society. Later, when Rumer was in New York working on a play, she missed her two dogs so much that she ended up visiting a pet store where she spotted Zhu Zhu. "She looked like she had never been held and I knew that I had to take her home and give her love."

Oprah Winfrey, Luke (a.k.a. Wonder Boy), and Sadie As a young girl, Oprah Winfrey bought her very first dog, a cockapoo mix, from a dog pound with her school lunch money and named him Simone. Since her first pound puppy, she has raised twenty-one dogs (eleven at one time on a farm in Indiana). She refers to her pack (currently of five) as "family members with fur" and says she is the happiest and most content in life walking on a trail through the woods with her dogs.

Luci Woodley and Sissy When she read that an animal farm in South Dakota was closing down and puppies urgently needed homes, Luci Woodley, a business consultant, flew one of them to her home in California. Luci was going through a very difficult time in her life when Sissy (7) came to her in 2005. Since then, Sissy, a poodle mix, has only brought light and happiness to Luci, who says, "she made me a better person."

Kimi Culp

Kimi Culp's unique specialty is generating original ideas and concepts and bringing them to life across multiple media platforms. Her experience includes work as a producer and story developer for *NBC Nightly News with Tom Brokaw*, ABC's *Good Morning America*, *20/20*, and *The Oprah Winfrey* Show. She is a partner at Long Story Short Media, a production and creative consulting company. Based in Los Angeles, she loves spending time with her husband and two children, hiking, and playing at the beach.

Lisa Erspamer

Lisa Erspamer, a dog lover since birth, most recently served as chief creative officer and executive vice president of programming and development for OWN: The Oprah Winfrey Network. Prior to working at OWN, Lisa served as co-executive producer of *The Oprah Winfrey Show*, where she produced and oversaw hundreds of shows including the biggest flash mob in history, the legendary car giveaway, Oprah's after-Oscar specials, Whitney Houston's final interview, and many others. Lisa currently lives in Los Angeles with her precious Yorkie, Lily. Lisa dedicates this book to her beloved boy, Louis, who sadly passed away in August 2012.

Robin Layton: Acknowledgments

I am overwhelmed with gratitude to the following people who helped make this book happen:

Lisa—You are one of the most amazing persons I know. You see things that others don't and allow us to dream a bigger dream. You'll never know how very grateful I am for all you've done for me, but especially for believing in me.

Kimi—You are a class act. You are a combination of brilliance and grace. Being in the trenches with you has been an experience I'll always treasure. You make everything better, including me.

Kessie "Prez"—I still think you should run for president. You keep us all organized and on top of things. Your countless hours of work are beyond appreciated. You are the mom of our team. No matter how much we had on our decks, you always said, "Give it to me, I'll do it."

Jen—Every thought and idea you had for this project was filled with kindness and love. Your positive attitude is contagious and has made such a difference.

Sara—Thanks for all the heavy lifting. Your humor kept me going and your maturity kept me grounded. Traveling together was an adventure! Thanks for driving, even when you couldn't reach the pedals.

Peggy—Thanks for occupying the best intentions, inspiration, and support for this project.

Susan "Snug"—Thanks for letting us use your Lincoln Town Car, Abe.

Mark and Brian, Andrea, Julie, Kimi, Linda, and Tyson—Thanks for your hospitality while I was shooting this book.

My parents, Shirley and Barrett Crump—Everything I do, I do to honor you.

Shakti—Thanks to my amazing partner for believing in me. I've never met anyone as unselfish as you, as supportive as you, as loving as you. You help me be the best me that I can be. I love you.

Monkey and Bella—Thanks to our dogs. The love we have for you is not possible to put in words (although we have tried!); it's immeasurable. Thanks for letting us be yours.

THE HUMANE SOCIETY
OF THE UNITED STATES

The *A Letter To My Dog* team supports the wonderful work of The Humane Society of the United States, and wishes to express gratitude for all of The HSUS's support with this project. To find out more about The Humane Society of the United States, or to donate, visit www.humanesociety.org.

Associate Editor: Jennifer Duck
Project Coordinator: Kessie Hollister
Photo Assistant to Robin Layton: Sara Gainey
Special thanks from the *A Letter to My Dog* team to Peggy Fitzsimmons for her endless love and support.

ISBN: 978-1-4521-1442-2

Produced and originated by PQ Blackwell Limited
116 Symonds Street, Auckland, New Zealand
www.pqblackwell.com

First published in the United States in 2012 by
Chronicle Books LLC.

Library of Congress Cataloging-in-Publication Data available.

Chronicle Books LLC
680 2nd Street
San Francisco, California 94107

Printed by 1010 Printing International Limited